Equity Partnerships

This book is dedicated to the generations of families who fought for their children to have equal rights in schools. Thank you for making a change. We'll continue to honor you by intentionally challenging the educational system.

I dedicate this book in memory of three of my nephews, James M. (Junior) Clark, Jr., Gregory V. Lewis, and Kenneth W. Clark. The joy you brought to our family was indescribable. You are greatly missed.

Angela

To Lee K. Smith—My sister, my friend—and to the educators and community members of Santa Maria, California.

Randy

This book is dedicated to the parents and families who have been ignored in the education process of their children—may they continue to fight for the education of their children.

Reyes

I am dedicating this book to my daughters, Jordyn and Kiera. I am so blessed by your presence in my life.

Cynthia

Equity Partnerships

A Culturally Proficient Guide to Family, School, and Community Engagement

Angela R. Clark-Louque, Randall B. Lindsey, Reyes L. Quezada, and Cynthia L. Jew

Foreword by Trudy T. Arriaga

FOR INFORMATION:

Corwin

A SAGE Company

2455 Teller Road

Thousand Oaks, California 91320

(800) 233-9936

www.corwin.com

SAGE Publications Ltd.

1 Oliver's Yard

55 City Road

London EC1Y 1SP

United Kingdom

SAGE Publications India Pvt. Ltd.

B 1/I 1 Mohan Cooperative Industrial Area

Mathura Road, New Delhi 110 044

India

SAGE Publications Asia-Pacific Pte. Ltd.

18 Cross Street #10-10/11/12

China Square Central

Singapore 048423

Program Director and Publisher: Dan Alpert

Content Development Editor: Lucas Schleicher

Senior Editorial Assistant: Mia Rodriguez

Production Editor: Tori Mirsadjadi

Copy Editor: Tammy Giesmann

Typesetter: C&M Digitals (P) Ltd.

Proofreader: Scott Oney

Indexer: Wendy Allex

Cover Designer: Janet Kiesel

Marketing Manager: Maura Sullivan

Printed in the United States of America

ISBN 978-1-5443-2415-9

This book is printed on acid-free paper.

Certified Chain of Custody
Promoting Sustainable Forestry
www.sfiprogram.org
SFI-01268

SFI label applies to text stock

19 20 21 22 23 10 9 8 7 6 5 4 3 2 1

DISCLAIMER: This book may direct you to access third-party content via web links, QR codes, or other scannable technologies, which are provided for your reference by the author(s). Corwin makes no guarantee that such third-party content will be available for your use and encourages you to review the terms and conditions of such third-party content. Corwin takes no responsibility and assumes no liability for your use of any third-party content, nor does Corwin approve, sponsor, endorse, verify, or certify such third-party content.

Contents

Visit the companion website at
http://resources.corwin.com/CPPartnerships
for downloadable resources.

Foreword

" *The only parents who were here were those who did not need to be here.*" As a teacher in the 1980s, a principal in the 1990s, and a superintendent from 2001 to 2015, I often heard that statement the day after a poorly attended evening event designed for parents by staff. This passive statement put the responsibility on the parent as the limited view of family and allowed educators to critique from the outside rather than give a culturally proficient response from the inside. What I did not hear was an analysis of why parents were not in attendance. Real-world barriers such as the time of day, lack of child care, cost of dinner, lack of transportation, language of the presentation, or simply lack of relevance in the topic that was decided on by staff could have contributed to the lack of parent involvement. Dialoguing about what families and communities need in alignment with the needs of educators was an outstanding starting point to family, school, and community engagement. I recall a family math night I was involved in as an elementary principal being very poorly attended. Rather than critique and complain, we asked questions and listened. The families informed us that a sewing class would be an engagement event they would attend. Learning to change the oil in a car would be useful. Immigration information in a safe, secure environment would be appreciated. We soon found ourselves with family events that were standing room only. We listened, we engaged, and we responded by removing the barriers.

We know inherently that parent involvement is critical to the success of our students. The Guiding Principles of Cultural Proficiency define family as the primary system of support in the education of children. Clark-Louque, Lindsey, Quezada, and Jew challenge educators to examine the extent to which we know how cultural groups define family and the manner in which we respond. We are not always clear about how to create culturally inclusive ways of engaging families in support of student engagement and achievement. *Equity Partnerships: A Culturally Proficient Guide to Family, School, and Community Engagement* clearly articulates the difference between parental involvement and family, school, and community engagement. Family engagement does not equate to parental involvement, and thus the terms should not be used interchangeably. Family engagement is an all-inclusive, shared responsibility and engages families to be actively supportive partners in meaningful ways. This is a very different concept from parental involvement in the days of volunteering, fundraising, and chaperoning by mostly mothers who did not work outside the home. The actions were limited in their scope of inclusivity and were generally part of a school- or district-driven agenda. The image of European American homes with families that include one mother, one father, and their children is a narrow view of family. Culturally proficient educators acknowledge families of all configurations to include single parent families, stepparents, multi-generational families, same-gender parents, foster care families, and other caregivers. The book challenges us to reframe our thinking and create new responses to lead us from parental involvement to the richness of family, school, and community engagement. The inside-out process highlighted in this book provides the reader with the opportunity to reflect on our own practices as we learn concepts and strategies for engaging families and communities through the lens of Cultural Proficiency. The tools of Cultural Proficiency are enhanced through the framing of the work around the research of Dr. Joyce Epstein, Dr. Steve Constantino, and Dr. Karen Mapp.

Throughout the book, Clark-Louque, Lindsey, Quezada, and Jew drive home the concept of family engagement in a culturally proficient environment using the Tools of Cultural Proficiency. Cultural Proficiency is a lens through which all family engagement is viewed and an opportunity to reflect on your assumptions and values for working with diverse families and communities. The guiding principles of Cultural Proficiency provide the moral framework to examine and align your district's values, policies, procedures, and practices. The approach of family engagement expects that all educators will be working in harmony with families to ensure that each learner and their family is valued and honored for the gifts they bring to the table.

Family, school, and community engagement is an integral component of education reform in the United States. Clark-Louque, Lindsey, Quezada, and Jew have provided a historical timeline of the progress we have made as a nation toward equity and inclusion and that which remains to be reached. Education reforms that focus only on classrooms and schools are leaving out the critical component of family, school, and community partnership, essential for long-term impact. When families, communities, and schools work in partnership, students are more successful academically and demonstrate increased social-psychological success, and, ultimately, the entire community benefits. Dropout rates decrease, attendance increases, and connectedness to school soars. The success associated with family, school, and community engagement occurs regardless of parents' education, income, language, or background. The intersection and impact of family, community, and parent engagement are factors we can control. Raising the next generation is a shared responsibility and privilege. The authors of this book have been first responders for decades by promoting Cultural Proficiency as a means to ensure equity and access for all. They have identified the powerful and critical link of family, school, and community engagement to strengthen families, build community support, and increase student success.

Trudy T. Arriaga, EdD
Coauthor, *Opening Doors: An Implementation*
Template for Cultural Proficiency
Associate Dean for Equity and Outreach,
California Lutheran University
Retired Superintendent, Ventura Unified
School District, California

Acknowledgments

Writing a book comes with a myriad of people supporting the project behind the scenes. This has become a reality because of the support, sacrifice, and encouragement we've all been given.

We'd like to thank our editors Dan Alpert and Lucas Schleicher for their patience and guidance throughout this book publishing project.

From Angela:

I thank God for His guidance throughout this process. My husband Gene, my son Nicholas, a young man of valor, and my daughter Gena, a young woman of faith and soft, yet strong determination, continue to inspire me. My mother, Glennie Bridgforth Clark, gives me laughter in her "old" age. Thank you for telling me over and over again the value of an education. You were right (again)!

My brother Joseph and his wife, Marsheila, are two of my strongest supporters and encourage me to live my best life. My dearest sister, Dr. Patricia Layne Clark, has taught me what unconditional compassion is. Because she's sacrificed her personal and professional life and chosen to live with and take care of our 88-year-old mother for the past four years, I am able to do what I do. Thank you for your infinite selflessness. My sister Anita L. Clark reminds me to shine. My nieces, Felicia Clark Bratcher, Shelbia Clark, Linda Clark Woods, and nephews Jon B. Clark and Dwight Clark have continuously told me they're proud of me. To my nieces, Dr. Christy Clark, Dr. Andrea M. Lewis Miller, and Sandra Clark Vaughn: thank you for your inspiration, encouragement, and unconditional love.

A heartfelt thank you for support with this manuscript to my mentors and friends, Randy and Delores Lindsey, who have advised, supported, and guided me throughout this entire process. Thank you for sharing this journey with me. Your support means more than words can express.

Dr. Gail L. Thompson, an exemplary author, friend, and prayer partner, always encourages me to write, and reminds me of my worth and how valuable my experiences are. Thank you for always encouraging me and praying for me. Janine Kremlin and Andria Sigler are my secret weapons, my prayer warriors. I so appreciate you in my life. Thank you for being a part of this book journey. To Constance Butler, Veronica Horton, Glenn A. Hill, Sr., Catherine Snow, Dr. Stanley L. Swartz, and Rose Vaxter, thank you for being a part of this book journey.

I'm grateful to the Bismark Street and Vaal Avenue community of Eunice Spencer, Cheryl Ballard, Rita and Regina "Cookie" Drake, Howard Applewhite, Wendell "Jig" Bills, Arthur "Moose" Franklin, Frederick "Doc" Johnson, Clarence "Foxx" Payne, Andre Steele, Michael Gant, and Bernard "Goo Daddy" Stanton. Thank you for helping me keep my mother and sister safe. A girl couldn't have a better neighbor-"hood" watch.

My co-authors and I have been saying we were going to write a book together for over 15 years . . . well, we've done it!

From Reyes:

I want to acknowledge my wife Cynthia who continues to support me in my education, as well as my father and mother who always believed in me in making this world a better place. To my son Raymundo Reyes and my daughter Kristina Belen who continue to be "Social Justice Warriors" in their own right as a community college professor and as a bilingual college counselor. Last, to my brothers and sisters whose unconditional support and love I have received all of these years.

From Cindy:

I wish to acknowledge Santa Clarita Valley International Charter School. The school community consisting of administrators, teachers, staff, students, and parents have been our school partners in Jordyn's school success. I am personally grateful to Dawn Evenson, Amber Raskin, the entire student support team, and Gris Ibarra to whom I am eternally grateful for holding my child's hand through this process.

PUBLISHER'S ACKNOWLEDGMENTS

Corwin gratefully acknowledges the contributions of the following reviewers:

Paul France
Third Grade Teacher
Latin School of Chicago
Chicago, IL

Young-chan Han
Educator
Maryland State Department of Education
Baltimore, MD

Tamara L. Huff
Family and Community Engagement Specialist
Wichita Public Schools
Wichita, KS

Andrea Phillip Hughes
Supervisor, ESSA and Title I Department
Prince George County Public Schools
Upper Marlboro, MD

Laura Metcalfe
Director, Early College Programs and Community Outreach
Mesa Community College
Mesa, AZ

Jael Ovalle
Program Manager, Parent Education
Los Angeles County Office of Education
Downey, CA

About the Authors

Dr. Angela R. Clark-Louque is Professor and Department Chair of Educational Leadership and Technology at California State University, San Bernardino. She has served as Associate Dean of Academic Affairs, Director of Graduate Studies, Department Chair of Doctoral Studies, Director of Educational Administration, and Director of Teacher Education. Her leadership has focused on urban educational leadership, developing organizational and community engagement capacity, and building a culture of equity. Prior to these roles, she served as a counselor and mathematics faculty at the community college level, and as an administrator and mathematics, social sciences, and band instructor at the high school level.

Dr. Clark-Louque earned her doctorate in Educational Leadership from Pepperdine University, an MA in Counseling from Loyola Marymount University (LMU), and a BA in Psychology from the University of California, Los Angeles (UCLA).

Dr. Clark-Louque's teaching and research focuses on equitable and culturally proficient practices for leaders, African American family engagement and student achievement, human resources, policy development, and governance. Her research activities include several peer-reviewed publications, grants, and reports, as well as international and national presentations and consulting workshops. Her most recent coauthored publications are "Race-neutral doesn't work: Black males' achievement, engagement, and school climate perceptions" (*Urban Education*, 2018) and "Cultural capital in the village: The role Black families play in the education of children" (*Journal of Multicultural Education*, 2014).

She co-authored the book *Exposing the "Culture of Arrogance" in the Academy: A Blueprint for Increasing Black Faculty Satisfaction in Higher Education"* (2005) with Dr. Gail L. Thompson and served as editor of the *Journal of Urban Learning, Teaching, and Research* through the American Educational Research Association (AERA).

She is a recipient of the Transformational Leadership Consortium, Outstanding Faculty in Research and Scholarly Activities, and Outstanding Faculty in

Instructionally-Related Activities Awards, and is a graduate Thomas Lakin Institute for Mentored Leadership—a national network of African American Community College CEOs. She has served as the committee chair of political activism for the NAACP and served on the *Los Angeles Committee of Honor* for the *Freedom's Sisters* exhibit and tour at the Simon Wiesenthal's Museum of Tolerance, which pays homage to a group of extraordinary African American women who have shaped the spirit and substance of civil rights in America.

She is a native of Memphis, Tennessee, and a graduate of George Washington Carver High School.

Randall B. Lindsey is Emeritus Professor at California State University, Los Angeles. He has served as a teacher, an administrator, executive director of a non-profit corporation, as Interim Dean at California Lutheran University, as Distinguished Educator in Residence at Pepperdine University, and as Chair of the Education Department at the University of Redlands. Prior to that, he served for seventeen years at California State University, Los Angeles in the Division of Administration and Counseling. All of Randy's experiences have been in working with diverse populations and his area of study is the behavior of White people in multicultural settings. His PhD is in Educational Leadership from Georgia State University, his Master of Arts in Teaching is in History Education from the University of Illinois, and his BS in Social Science Education is from Western Illinois University. He has served as a junior high school and high school teacher and as an administrator in charge of school desegregation efforts. At Cal State, L.A. he served as Chair of the Division of Administration and Counseling and as Director of the Regional Assistance Centers for Educational Equity, a regional race desegregation assistance center. With co-authors he has written several books and articles on Cultural Proficiency. His most recent publication is *The Cultural Proficiency Manifesto: Finding Clarity Amidst the Noise.*

Reyes Quezada, EdD, is a professor in the Department of Learning and Teaching at University of San Diego. Dr. Quezada writes and teaches in the areas of Bilingual Education, K–12 Teacher Recruitment, Issues on Faculty of Color, Instructional Models, Home-School Community Partnerships, Experiential Education, and Physical Education Through Adventure Based Programs. He came to University of San Diego in 1999 from the University of Redlands and prior to that he taught at California State University, Stanislaus. He has also lectured for California State University San Bernardino, San Diego State University, and the Washington Center for Academic Seminars in Washington, D.C. Among his articles are "K–12 Teacher Recruitment: Implications for Teacher Education" (*Teacher Education Quarterly*), co-authored with Angela R. Clark-Louque; "Developing Diverse Faculty in Culturally Proficient Education Programs" (*Journal of Multicultural Education*); and "Forming Home-School Community Partnerships Among Bilingual Communities" (*The School Community Journal*).

He has co-authored two other books on Cultural Proficiency as well as book chapters on the same topic. He was the co-chair for the California Commission on Teacher Credentialing Committee on Accreditation (COA), sits on two national boards of directors—the Council on Accreditation for Educator Preparation Programs (CAEP), the American Association for Colleges of Teacher Education (AACTE), and chairs one international organization—the International Council for the Education of Teachers (ICET).

Cynthia L. Jew, PhD, is a professor at California Lutheran University in Thousand Oaks, California. Dr. Jew teaches in the Counselor Education program focusing on Field Experiences and School Systems as she prepares School Counselors. She is co-author of *Culturally Proficient Inquiry: A Lens for Identifying and Examining Education Gaps* (Corwin, 2008) and *Culturally Proficient Schools: All Means All* (Corwin, 2017). She also serves as a consultant to the Santa Clarita Valley International Charter schools focusing on the areas of Student Support and Inclusiveness. She is a Licensed Psychologist and Certified School Psychologist. She has two daughters: Jordyn, who is deaf and wears cochlear implants, and Kiera.

Introduction

In thinking of any strong and positive relationship, one's thoughts might include the effort, commitment, and work that are involved in maintaining the relationship. In time, several other factors may emerge to make the relationship strong and make the relationship last. This book was conceived and designed to intentionally focus our efforts as educators on inclusive ways to engage the diverse communities served by our schools. Mostly, this book is about relationship building with the communities that entrust their children and youth to us.

This book has two key features. The book is structured to provide opportunities to learn concepts and strategies for engaging families and communities through a lens of culturally proficient relationship building. And, the book is structured to provide you, the reader, frequent opportunities to reflect on your own practice and to engage colleagues in dialogue for considering your school or district's policies and practices relative to community engagement. The chapters present foundational concepts from the prominent literature on family and community engagement through the lens of the Cultural Proficiency Framework.

Ms. Kaya Henderson, the current leader of the Global Learning Lab for Community Impact at Teach for All, recently wrote a blog titled *We Don't Need Saviors, We Need Leaders Who Are Ready to Form True Partnerships With Families and Communities*. In her blog, she recalls an experience as chancellor of the Washington D.C. Public Schools working with the city council to alleviate the chronic issues of student truancy and absenteeism. Here's an excerpt from her story:

> *My last job was as chancellor of the District of Columbia Public Schools, and one of the predominant lessons I took away from that position was a renewed appreciation for how many factors influence whether a student learns at school. I'm talking about a family's economic stability, I'm talking about housing, I'm talking about health care, and a host of other intersecting issues.*
>
> *Case in point: One school year, we were challenged by the City Council to improve outrageously high truancy rates in some of our most challenging schools across the city. Obviously, if students aren't showing up to school at all or on time, they don't stand a chance to learn. The Council wanted to enact legislation to punish students and families with high truancy rates. I asked the councilmembers if they had ever asked students why they didn't come to school. It was a radical idea that nobody had tried. So, I gathered our most truant students at our two most challenging high schools, and over breakfast and lunch, asked them why their attendance was poor.*
>
> *They cited a number of reasonable explanations, but the most prevalent was that by the middle of the month, they were out of money to pay for transportation*

to school. From that, we were able to work with the transit authority, City Council, and the mayor to fund the Kids Ride Free Program, guaranteeing free bus and train transportation to school for all of our students across the city. As a result, we saw significant increases in attendance.

Source: Henderson, Kaya (2018). "We Don't Need Saviors, We Need Leaders Who Are Ready to Form True Partnerships With Families and Communities." Education Post. https://educationpost .org/we-dont-need-saviors-we-need-leaders-who-are-ready-to-form-true-partnerships-with-families- and-communities/

This is just one example to demonstrate the intersection and impact of family, school, and community working and problem solving together for the benefit of students. Each stakeholder has an integral role to play in the academic success of children and schools. Just think for a moment that had Chancellor Henderson not posed her suggestion to the city council, punitive actions toward students might have taken place. Engaging members of the community, whether parents, students, or other community members, has the potential for powerful stories to be shared and for educators and community members to work together in addressing issues that affect students' equitable access to educational experiences.

A feature of this book is the presentation of real-world barriers experienced by schools and their communities and the manner in which the barriers were reduced and sometimes eliminated through culturally proficient educator actions that led to engagement. You will learn how to use the Tools of Cultural Proficiency to reflect on your assumptions and values for working with diverse communities, and also how to work with colleagues to co-create systemic practices and policies to devise, implement, and assess family and community engagement actions in your schools and districts.

OVERVIEW OF THE CHAPTERS

The Cultural Proficiency Framework serves as a readily accessible conceptual base that provides guidance in examining and aligning your school or district's core values, policies, and practices in ways that are inclusive of the diverse communities you serve. The book presents the moral, legal, and educational context in which US schools exist as opportunities for schools to engage the broadest constituency of families and communities served by your school or district. You may find familiar the vignettes that represent challenges faced by educators. Each challenging vignette is followed by a vignette that demonstrates culturally proficient family, school, and community engagement.

Lastly, this book provides strategies for developing your own action plans and a list of selected resources drawn from respected authors and programs. Along with the Cultural Proficiency Framework, each chapter provides reflective questions to guide your own educational journey as well as dialogic questions and activities to guide professional discussions among your colleagues in developing inclusive approaches to family and community engagement.

In *Chapter 1*, The Cultural Proficiency Framework composed of its four tools is described—Overcoming Barriers, Guiding Principles, The Continuum, and

Essential Elements. The Tools are a means for addressing educational inequities. A Cultural Proficiency Family and Community Engagement Rubric is included to provide focus and guidance for moving from exclusion to benign neglect to participation.

Chapter 2 poses and addresses the *why* question of the need for educators and families and communities to engage in a manner that assures access, inclusivity, and equitable outcomes for all students. What parents and families say they want from schools, and how they'd like to be engaged, is a focal point of the chapter.

Chapter 3 provides a historical timeline of the legal mandates that have evolved in a way that supports family and community engagement. A quick journey from the colonial United States to landmark Supreme Court decisions and the Elementary and Secondary Education Act to the current Every Student Succeeds Act (ESSA) are briefly described to provide a perspective on the progress we have made as a country for continuing on the journey to equity and inclusion.

Chapter 4 frames our work around three prominent and widely respected family and community-based authors as the foundation for our work in partnering with families: John Hopkins University professor Dr. Joyce Epstein and the Six Types of Involvement; former acting Virginia Superintendent of Public Instruction, Dr. Steve Constantino's 5 Simple Principles; and Harvard Graduate School of Education Senior Lecturer Dr. Karen Mapp and Dr. Paul Kuttner's Dual Capacity Building Framework. Taken together, these frameworks guided the manner in which we infused their work into the Cultural Proficiency Framework. We align their research-based approaches with the Essential Elements of Cultural Proficiency to derive engagement principles that are indicative of inclusive family, school, and community engagement strategies.

In *Chapter 5*, we pose seven evidenced-based family engagement skills and concepts to enhance capacity building toward equitable relationships: communication, collaboration, compassion-caring, culture, connection, community, and collective responsibility. Epstein's, Constantino's, and Mapp and Kuttner's approaches are paired with the Cultural Proficiency Framework to illustrate building effective and school-community partnerships inclusive of diverse communities.

Chapter 6 focuses on authors' descriptions of challenging experiences schools face while interacting with their communities. Vignettes of cross-cultural barriers are presented and analyzed in a manner for you to deepen your understanding and use of the Tools of Cultural Proficiency and, at the same time, to reflect on your practice and that of your school or district.

Chapter 7 focuses on authors' descriptions of successes that grew out of the challenges described in Chapter 6. The situations provide insight into the array of interactions, communications, and expectations that foster challenging and constructive interactions between schools and families. The focus for each vignette is on the intentionality of school personnel with community constituents in ways that valued their participation and that ensured participation in constructive decisions that affected their children and youth.

Chapter 8 focuses on committing to action in working with the diverse communities served by your school or district. You will have opportunities to apply the Tools of Cultural Proficiency and the 7 Cs in the form of preassessments and strategies to strengthen your commitment and guide you and your colleagues through the initial development of a Cultural Proficiency Equity Action Plan.

Chapter 9 challenges readers to make connections with their own schools by presenting learning strategies. The chapter serves as a resource guide to facilitate engaging activities for schools, parents, families, educators, community members and organizations, and school leaders.

RESOURCES

The book concludes with resources and a book study guide for educators to use as their journey continues in securing access, equity, and inclusion to family, schools, and communities. The book study guide is structured to be used by individuals as a guide for exploring their values and behaviors when working with diverse communities. The book provides guidance for school teams as they examine and revise school or district policies and practices that foster access and equitable outcomes.

PART I

The Basics of Cultural Proficiency and Engagement

The Cultural Proficiency Framework

TOOLS FOR FAMILY, SCHOOL, AND COMMUNITY ENGAGEMENT

Go and get yourself an education. Once you do,
no one can ever take it away from you.
—GLENNIE BRIDGEFORTH CLARK, 1960, EVERY PAGE OF MY LIFE

Vignette

WHAT IS YOUR STRAWBERRY FIELD?

I was at my desk preparing to edit a nearly complete manuscript when I heard my cell phone buzzing. I recognized the phone number as belonging to the assistant principal of Santa Maria High School. Looking forward to what he might have to say about the good work under way at the high school, I said my requisite *Hello!* to which he responded with a question: *Guess where we are?* Since it was Tuesday about 10 a.m., I responded with, *You are somewhere on campus?* I was wrong. In the merriest of voices, he proclaimed, *Three of us are out in the strawberry fields to meet parents.*

Having been to Santa Maria numerous times, I was well aware of the extensive strawberry fields in the area and knew that many parents were employed both in year round and in seasonal jobs. In Chapters 6 and 7, you will learn more about the levels of community engagement present in Santa Maria and how they are turning systemic barriers into opportunities for constructive engagement with community members.

If you are like us, you may have already turned ahead to Chapters 6 and 7 to find out how the strawberry field experience turned out. Not a problem if you do so. Once that curiosity is satisfied, we hope you are motivated to return here and to proceed through this book in more or less traditional fashion. In doing so, you will learn about the Cultural Proficiency Framework and the manner in which the Tools of Cultural Proficiency are being applied in at least three additional settings.

The Cultural Proficiency Framework is composed of a set of tools—Overcoming Barriers, Guiding Principles, Continuum, and Essential Elements—which, taken together, provide a foundation for powerful professional learning applied to the intersecting topics of diversity, inclusivity, and equity. Learning and applying the Tools provides a means for addressing inequities that exist within our education profession and institutions as well as in our general society. Today's generation did not create these inequities; however, clearly, they are on our doorstep to address.

We, the authors, believe that addressing systemic inequities is the calling issued by Cross, Bazron, Dennis, and Isaacs (1989) and Fullan (2003) and is addressed in this and other Cultural Proficiency books, as well as those of other prominent equity authors.

In this chapter, we provide a description of each of the Tools of Cultural Proficiency and then arrange the Tools into a rubric. The rubric demonstrates the application of the Tools to parent, family, school, and community engagement. As with any other rubrics, the rubric in this chapter is intended as an assessment, *not* an evaluative tool. In other words, and we will repeat this phrase often, the professional use of the rubric is *to inform, not to indict.*

Should you desire a deeper discussion of the Tools of Cultural Proficiency, you will want to consult *The Manual for School Leadership,* 4th edition (Lindsey, Nuri-Robins, Terrell, & Lindsey, 2018). Resource A of this book provides a brief description of other Cultural Proficiency titles along with the essential questions which each book addresses. No matter which Cultural Proficiency title you select, the same four tools are applied. Each title presents a specific context, more nuanced description of how the Tools are applied in teaching, counseling, professional learning communities, coaching, schools as organizational entities, impoverished and low-income communities, LGBT communities, migrant communities, and English learning classrooms among other communities and contexts.

FIGURE 1.1
Tools to Cultural Proficiency

- **Guiding Principles**
- **Overcoming the Barriers**
- **Continuum**
- **5 Essential Elements**

Source: Center for Culturally Proficient Educational Practice, 2018

OVERCOMING THE BARRIERS TO CULTURAL PROFICIENCY

Recognizing and confronting inequities that exist and persist in our schools and society in general is a level of awareness basic to successful use of the Tools. Cross et al. (1989) identified these basic obstacles as a Tool they called Barriers:

- **Systemic Oppression.** Inequities that continue to exist and persist because of past and present policies and practices in organizations and society are evidence of a system of oppression. These policies and practices guide the behaviors of members of organizations and many people in communities. Although individual employees may not intend to discriminate against other individuals, the power structure of organizations and the rules and regulations function, whether by intent or not, to keep some groups invisible while others benefit from the structure. School districts, for example, are often designed to serve some students well because they have always been served well, while at the same time, historically marginalized groups continue to be underserved or need to be served differently.

- **Sense of Entitlement.** When individuals or members of some organizations believe they have acquired all the personal achievements and societal benefits solely on the basis of their merits, hard work, and character, they may be unaware of a larger system of entitlement and privilege that supported their accomplishments and status in society. Individuals may not realize that along with this sense of entitlement comes a commitment and responsibility to reorder any perquisites they may have. Educators and families today did not create the systems of oppression and privilege, but they are here for us to address and dismantle today.

- **Unawareness of the Need to Adapt.** When members of the dominant group in schools fail to recognize the need to make personal and organizational changes to meet the needs of the school community, they may also fail to see any problems that might exist with cross-cultural communications and interactions within the community. Educators must constantly monitor and assess the changing demographics of the community as well as assess the needs of the students. Individuals who are unaware of the need to adapt often see any issues that arise from diverse perspectives as the *other people's problem*. Typically, the *newcomers* to the school community are invisible to the dominant group until concerns arise; then the focus becomes an *us vs. them* blame game, rather than asking, *How might we work together as a culturally proficient community?*

- **Resistance to Change.** Many families and educators are satisfied with the way things are, rather than seeking to change the way things are done. This behavior is a natural resistance to change. Even when some student groups are not served well, as evidenced by the education gap, many educators would prefer serving most students the way they have always taught and led. However, in 2001, the calculations for acknowledging or ignoring achievement disparities changed to never be the same again. The passage of No Child Left Behind (NCLB), a reauthorization of the 1965 Elementary and Secondary Education Act (ESEA), has provided school leaders the *opportunity* to examine student achievement data and disaggregate by demographic groups. The word *opportunity* is so highlighted to point out that the National Association for Educational Progress (NAEP) had been issuing biannual reports for two decades that were too often ignored or minimized by local educators and educational policy makers. NCLB provided a means for moving the examination of achievement data from *opportunity* to an *expectation* that paved a pathway for addressing issues of inequity.

Education leaders now look for ways to examine data for inequities and develop actions to better serve all students. Resistance to change may be natural and normal, but in our communities today, ignoring inequities is no longer acceptable.

The Barriers manifest themselves in our schools and communities. Families who are served well by their educators and schools often do not encounter these obstacles or are totally unaware of them, because the barriers are invisible. Other community members face and are challenged by these barriers on a regular basis and wonder why others do not experience them. Barriers, when left undetected or not responded to, *function* as default core values. Core values drive our behaviors. In other words, our values are our *why*. Our behaviors are our *what*. The actions of educators toward students and their families are the manifestations of the values they hold about teaching and learning. Educators who view some students as *less than* other students because of their cultures and socioeconomic backgrounds embrace deficit-laden values. In such environments, educators see targeted students as coming from lesser cultures and socioeconomic circumstances—the approach to which is schools that must rectify the deficiencies caused by membership in a lesser culture or socioeconomic circumstance, whereas educators who believe they can teach all students hold values that allow them to see students as having assets and cultural attributes upon which educators can build successful educational experiences for students.

Knowing and identifying the Barriers requires educators and families to join together to learn about and value the students' home cultures as well as the school culture. Together, educators and families can share the values they hold for each student succeeding at levels higher than ever before. The Guiding Principles are a set of core values for overcoming the Barriers. The following section defines the Guiding Principles and describes how they work interdependently so that educators and families can confront and overcome the Barriers.

FIGURE 1.2
Barriers to Cultural Proficiency

- **Systemic Oppression**
- **A Sense of Entitlement**
- **Unawareness of Need to Adapt**
- **Resistance to Change**

Source: Center for Culturally Proficient Educational Practice, 2018

Reflection

As you read the descriptors of the Barriers, what are some challenges that you have faced or might face in engaging families in their children's education? What seems to be getting in the way of more educators engaging with families to support student relationships and achievement? What might be some insights you've gained from reading about and understanding the influence of the Barriers?

_____

_____

_____

_____

The Guiding Principles serve as core values to guide educators as they make teaching, learning, and leading decisions. These core values also guide members of organizations to establish, implement, and monitor school and district policies and practices. These individual behaviors must be focused on equity, access, diversity, and inclusion for all students and families. The Guiding Principles applied to family, school, and community engagement in Figure 1.3 include the following:

- *Principle: Culture is everywhere.* Culture is all around like the air around us. People are so used to culture, they don't notice it until it changes or is challenged by other groups' biases.

- *Principle: People are served differently by the culture in charge.* Everyone in the organization needs to know the rules and the policies and how they impact everyone.

- *Principle: People have group identities and personal identities.* We may want to be known and identified by our cultural ethnicity while at the same time show that we do not always fit all the descriptors of that group.

- *Principle: Diversity within cultural groups is important.* Within any one culture group are differences of income, education, faith, sexual orientation, and politics. Often profiles and stereotypes are built from assumptions that cultural groups are alike.

- *Principle: Each group has unique needs that must be valued and respected.* Each student who comes to our schools deserves to learn about the United States history and culture, even the parts that are difficult to understand, because of the dominant group's mistreatment and oppression of other groups. Be aware of lessons to learn from each other. Each student and all families deserve to learn about the history and culture of their country of origin. Through these collaborative learning experiences, families and educators value the unique needs of each student.

- *Principle: Families, as defined by their culture, are the primary support system for our students.* Our families describe who they are culturally and as a family. The school system does not define or describe who they are culturally or as a family.

- *Principle: Families must be bicultural.* Irrespective of the family culture, students and their families must understand the organizational culture of the school. Unless a family has grown up in US schools, they must learn the ways of the school.

- *Principle: Newcomers to our schools and communities must acknowledge, adjust to, and accept cross-cultural interactions as necessary social and communications dynamics.* Our families learn to reach out to educators and communities to learn communication and social norms to navigate successfully within the community. Our school members must reach out to assist in this process.

- *Principle: The school system must incorporate cultural knowledge into educational/school practices and policy making, and decisions within departments/divisions.* What do leaders and employees know about cultural shifts or demographic changes at school sites? How are some students served well while others are not served well or need to be served differently?

FIGURE 1.3

Guiding Principles for Family, School, and Community Engagement

- **Culture is a predominant force in shaping values, behaviors, and institutions' policies and practices.**
- **People are served in varying degrees by the dominant culture.**
- **There is diversity within and among cultures and both are important.**
- **Every group has unique culturally defined needs that must be respected.**
- **People have personal identities and group identities. The dignity of individuals is not guaranteed unless the dignity of their people is also preserved.**
- **The best of both worlds enhances the capacity of all.**
- **The family, as defined by each culture, is the primary system of support in the education of children.**
- **School systems must recognize that marginalized populations have to be at least bicultural and that this status creates a unique set of issues to which the system must be equipped to respond.**
- **Inherent in cross-cultural interactions are dynamics that must be acknowledged, adjusted to, and accepted.**

Source: Center for Culturally Proficient Educational Practice, 2018

Reflection

As you examine the Guiding Principles, what might be some insights that you have about core values that impact educators' decisions? What are the core values that guide your actions? Why do you do what you do? Engage in conversation with your colleagues about their core values and the core values that guide your school/district's leaders' actions?

_____

_____

_____

_____

The Continuum is the most visible of the tools. In our work with educators in their schools and districts, we have observed that one or more participants are familiar with the Continuum from previous books, articles, or workshops. Irrespective of participants' experiences with this Tool, we emphasize the Continuum has two distinct phases:

- *Cultural Destructiveness, Incapacity, and Blindness* are formed and informed by the Barriers serving as negative core values; and

- *Cultural Precompetence, Competence, and Proficiency* are formed and informed by the Guiding Principles serving as positive core values.

The first three points on the continuum may find us referring to our students as *underperforming*, while the next three points would find us referring to the ways in which we are *underserving* our students and their communities (i.e., an *inside-out* approach to examining assumptions that inform values and actions of educators and their schools). This distinction of underlying core values is an important bedrock to effective use of the Tools of Cultural Proficiency. The Continuum includes the following six points as representative of educators' behaviors based on their core values. Each point on the Continuum has a brief description.

- *Cultural Destructiveness*—seeking to eliminate vestiges of the cultures of others through negative and hostile actions and comments.

- *Cultural Incapacity*—seeking to make the culture of others appear to be wrong by dismissing and blaming them.

- *Cultural Blindness*—being unaware or pretending to not see or acknowledge the culture of others.

- *Cultural Precompetence*—becoming aware of what one doesn't know about working in diverse school communities. Moving forward in a positive, constructive direction or faltering, stopping, or possibly regressing.

- *Cultural Competence*—viewing one's personal and organizational work as an interactive arrangement in which the educator enters into diverse communities actively engaging with family cultural groups that are different from the educator. Committing to planning and implementing actions using the 5 Essential Elements of Cultural Competence.

- *Cultural Proficiency*—making the commitment to lifelong learning for the purpose of being increasingly effective in serving the educational needs of *all* cultural groups. Holding the vision of what can be and committing to assessments that serve as benchmarks on the road to student success. Advocating for equity, mentoring equity leaders, and marshaling resources to eliminate inequities through high quality professional learning experiences for educators and families.

FIGURE 1.4

The Cultural Proficiency Continuum for Family and Community Engagement

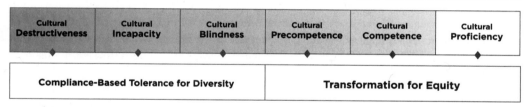

Cultural Destructiveness	Cultural Incapacity	Cultural Blindness	Cultural Precompetence	Cultural Competence	Cultural Proficiency

Compliance-Based Tolerance for Diversity	Transformation for Equity

Source: Center for Culturally Proficient Educational Practice, 2018

Reflection

As you examine the Continuum, what might be some insights that you have about core values that impact educators' behaviors? What sense are you making of the Continuum? In what ways does the Continuum align with the Barriers and Guiding Principles?

_____

_____

_____

_____

THE ESSENTIAL ELEMENTS OF CULTURAL PROFICIENCY

As in the old adage *All roads lead to Rome,* the function of the preceding tools is to lead us to a foundational appreciation of how the Tools give rise to actions. The first three Tools describe *why?* we do this work: (1) Identifying Barriers that get in the way of all students learning and achieving at high levels. (2) Knowing the core values that help us overcome those barriers that created many of the inequities our families and students face. (3) Closely monitoring and assessing our progress toward equity, access, and inclusion using the Continuum.

Now, we ask the questions *what?* do we do and *how?* do we do it. The final Tool, the Essential Elements, functions and serves as action standards for educators' values and beliefs and for school and district formulation and execution of policies and practices. Effective use of the Essential Elements is predicated on a deep understanding of the duality of Barriers vs. Guiding Principles and the associated language represented by the points along the Continuum. The 5 Essential Elements applied to family and community engagement are

- **Assessing Cultural Knowledge.** Being aware of what you know about your culture, the culture of the school community, others' cultures, how you react to others' cultures, and what you need to do to be effective in cross-cultural situations. Ask: *Who am I in relation to the community I serve? Who am I in relation to the cultural groups living in the school community? What more do I want to learn about the cultural communities in our service area?*

- **Valuing Diversity.** Making the effort to be inclusive of people whose viewpoints and experiences are different from yours. Demonstrate the value you hold for all cultural groups through conversations, decision making, and problem solving. Ask: *In what ways can each and every student see themselves in this school?*

- **Managing the Dynamics of Difference.** Viewing conflict as a natural and normal process that has cultural contexts. The dynamics of diversity can be taught, valued, understood, and used in managing resources, creative problem solving, and resolving conflict. Ask: *In what ways might we view our differences as our assets rather than our deficits? What structures and practices are in place to assist us in managing conflict and sharing ideas?*

- **Adapting to Diversity.** Having the will to learn about others and the skill and ability to use others' cultural experiences and backgrounds in educational settings. Being aware that change is natural, normal, and necessary for growth and progress. Ask: *In what ways might we provide opportunities for newcomers to share their assets and experiences with the community? What data will help us monitor and assess our growth and progress toward future plans? What is our future as a community?*

- **Institutionalizing Cultural Knowledge.** Making learning about cultural groups and their experiences and perspectives as an integral part of your ongoing learning. Ask: *What else do we need or want to know? Who else might join us as partners?*

FIGURE 1.5

The Essential Elements of Cultural Proficiency Family and Community Engagement

1. **Assessing Cultural Knowledge**

2. **Valuing Diversity**

3. **Managing the Dynamics of Difference**

4. **Adapting to Diversity**

5. **Institutionalizing Cultural Knowledge**

Source: Center for Culturally Proficient Educational Practice, 2018

As you examine the Essential Elements, what might be some insights that you have about actions for equity? What sense are you making of the 5 Essential Elements as the core verbs for an action plan? In what ways do Essential Elements align with the Continuum, the Barriers, and Guiding Principles? Now what?

_____

_____

_____

_____

THE FAMILY, SCHOOL, AND COMMUNITY ENGAGEMENT RUBRIC

The rubric brings together the Tools of Cultural Proficiency in a manner to operationalize their use in addressing issues and topics related to family, school, and community engagement. A few hints are appropriate for reading and "decoding" Table 1.1, The Family, School, and Community Engagement Rubric:

- *Take a few moments to locate the two large columns*—"Informed by Barriers to Cultural Proficiency" and "Informed by Guiding Principles of Cultural Proficiency."

- *Note that under Barriers are Continuum points*—Cultural Destructiveness, Incapacity, and Blindness.

- *Note that under Guiding Principles are Continuum points*—Cultural Precompetence, Competence, and Proficiency.

- *Now, turn your attention to the first column.* Each row presents an Essential Element with a descriptor of the essence of that element in terms of Parent, Family, and Community Engagement.

- *Next, select any one of the Elements and read from left to right.* Begin by reading the illustration of Family, School, and Community Engagement that is *Culturally Destructive* and across until you have read all six illustrations. You will note that negativity decreases and positivity increases when arriving at Cultural Precompetence and beyond.

- *Finally, note that the column titled Cultural Competence is shaded.* This indicates that the standard is met at this point. Cultural Proficiency is future focused in ways that anticipate and embrace challenges as opportunities for new and continuous learning.

TABLE 1.1

Family, School, and Community Engagement Rubric

	Informed by Barriers to Cultural Proficiency			Informed by Guiding Principles of Cultural Proficiency		
	Cultural Destructiveness	Cultural Incapacity	Cultural Blindness	Cultural Precompetence	Cultural Competence	Cultural Proficiency
Assessing Cultural Knowledge—extent to which community involvement facilitates the identification, assessment, and development of cultural identity	Ignore, intimidate, or punish the expression of needs of diverse parent/community groups.	Help culturally diverse family and community members by purposefully assimilating them into the dominant culture.	Family, community, and school leaders are from select communities without regard to different cultural groups.	Recognizing the importance of knowing about each other's cultures, family, community, and school leaders may learn about each other in authentic ways.	Family, community, and school leaders learn about each other's cultures in order to bridge the gaps between and among home, community, and school cultures.	Family, community, and school leaders continuously scan the environment in order to be responsive to ever-changing community demographics.
Valuing Diversity—extent to which parent and community diversity is valued	Actively prevent involvement of different cultural groups in making decisions about programs and services that meet the needs of all students.	Identify family and community members to remediate their cultural deficiencies.	Family and community involvement responsive to legal mandates without respect to different cultural groups.	Recognizing need to involve culturally diverse community groups in decision making, may include some but not all groups appropriately.	Involve representative constituencies of families and community members as partners in making decisions about programs and services that meet the needs of all students.	Representative constituencies of families and community members, advocate closing achievement gaps, and develop and model advocacy for social justice practices.

Managing the Dynamics of Difference—extent to which community involvement efforts develop the capacity to mediate cultural conflict between and among diverse family/community groups and the school.	Sabotage involvement of some family groups by instigating competition for scarce resources that results in intergroup conflict.	Ignore family and community groups that are working to address issues important to them.	Facilitate groups working together to find common ground on divisive issues.	Recognizing emerging intergroup conflict, staff and community leaders may develop conflict resolution strategies or identify key *liaisons* within diverse cultural groups.	Create a culture which encourages multiple perspectives and builds capacity for and dialogue between and among all community, family, and school groups.	Staff, family, and community groups work together to anticipate the needs of the ever-changing community and associated issues.
Adapting to Diversity—extent to which people and schools change to meet the needs of the community.	Families and school staff prevent changes intended to benefit culturally different community and student groups.	Families and school staff consider meeting the needs of culturally different groups as divisive.	Families and school staff do not acknowledge the need to meet the needs of culturally different community groups.	Recognizing differences between home and school cultures, family, community, and school leaders may begin to address needs of diverse community populations.	Families and school staff work together to identify and address needs of diverse cultural populations.	Staff, families, and community work together to meet the needs of all cultural groups and anticipate and plan for changes within the community.
Institutionalizing—extent to which people and schools integrate knowledge about diverse community and organizational cultures into daily practice.	School staff creates policies and practices that systematically exclude culturally different family groups from being involved in important decisions about the education of their children.	Changes to meet diverse student needs are seen as against the status quo and the assimilation of different cultural groups.	School staff supports and sponsors traditional family and community organizations and governmental mandates, believing they serve all cultural groups.	Recognizing family and community needs as they arise, and may develop structures to respond to the needs.	Creates structures that address the diverse cultural needs of the family, school, and community groups and assesses effectiveness in meeting those needs.	Family and community groups provide ongoing meaningful contributions to decisions, policies, and practices that serve the diverse needs of the community.

Reflection

What sense are you making of the Rubric? In what ways might you use the Rubric in your school/district? What are three key takeaways from this section about the Rubric?

_____

_____

_____

_____

Going Deeper Reflection

Now that you know the Tools of Cultural Proficiency, what might be some implications of the Tools in relation to the *inside-out* approach? What might be some assumptions, values, and beliefs on which this Framework is built?

_____

_____

_____

_____

Going Deeper Dialogic Questions

What might this "Framework in Action" look and sound like in your school or district? What would outsiders notice about family and community engagement strategies that are different from most schools? What are three takeaways from this chapter? In what ways might the Tool framework support a new Design Team or other creative work you are doing as a leadership team? What might your next steps be?

_____

_____

_____

_____

SUMMARY

The Tools of Cultural Proficiency exist as a design model to engage families and community partners with educators for transformative actions. Unfortunately, we educators typically develop action plans for others to implement. In other words, A Design Team for Family, School, and Community Engagement should include educators, parents, family members, community partners, *and* students to design the needs assessment, develop the outcomes, and determine the measures of success. Without these team members involved from the early design stage, the final product will be another compliance document based on wishful thinking and concluding with disappointing results. The Tools framework is a design grounded in positive assumptions and based on deeply held values for equity, inclusion, and diversity.

LOOKING AHEAD: CHAPTER 2

Chapter 2 begins a deep dive into the *why* of family, school, and community engagement. Terminology unique to the topic of family, school, and community engagement is presented. Benefits of engagement are discussed in terms of supporting student access and achievement. As an educator or involved parent, family, or community member, you are provided, as you are throughout this book, with opportunities to reflect on your values, thinking, and actions.

The *Why* of Engagement

Passing the baton of courage means teaching the next generation the courage to stand, even if you have to stand by yourself.

—DR. KENNETH C. ULMER, 2018, P. 33

Vignette

I'M ONLY HUMAN

Dear Principal (Dr.) Hayes,

This email is to inform you of a conversation that was held on 11/28/2017 at 3:15 p.m. between Valerie Coleman, Band Instructor at Carver High School, and Performing Arts Assistant/Pit Instructor Joseph Rankins, regarding the behavior of my daughter, Marvonna Baxter.

On 11/28/2017, at 11:10pm, Marvonna informed me that she had been asked to return to Ms. Coleman's class after school for a short meeting. During the meeting, my daughter was informed by Mr. Rankins that she would not be allowed to participate in the 2017–2018 Winter Drumline season due to her attitude problems. Marvonna indicated that she'd been spoken to about her attitude last year and she had made strides this year to make the requested attitude adjustments since then. Marvonna attempted to resolve the matter but was ultimately told she would not be allowed to participate.

As a result of the unfavorable outcome, I initiated a meeting with the band instructor, Ms. Coleman, to investigate further. It should be noted that until the evening of 11/28/2017, I've never been informed about Marvonna's (negative?) behavior, during marching or concert band by Ms. Coleman, my daughter's certified instructor for at least the last two school years.

To begin the meeting, I asked, "For clarification, what are the qualifications for auditioning for the Winter Drumline season?" Ms. Coleman informed me that you only needed to be a human being. This was perplexing to me because I'm sure my daughter meets the qualifications. She then continued to explain how over the last two years my daughter had been warned about her attitude. I noted that out of all the examples that were mentioned, they couldn't have been serious enough to jeopardize her participation in drumline, because none were expressed to me, the parent. Even if the totality of the behavior was enough to impede her participation, surely someone would think enough of the consequence to communicate with me, because otherwise, I'm thinking that my daughter is on the drumline her senior year.

I expressed my confusion because I've never received any calls or emails from Ms. Coleman over the past two years. When asked why I've never heard of these complaints prior to 11/28/2017, Ms. Coleman indicated she attempted to call me about a month ago. The comment seemed embellished as she never mentioned any incidents that occurred during the 2017–2018 band season. In fact, Ms. Coleman had nothing negative to say about Marvonna's recent behavior. Being that Ms. Coleman never addressed Marvonna's behavior problems to me when they allegedly occurred, I can only conclude that the comments mentioned during our conversation were to justify punishing her this year for behavior that happened during the 2016–2017 season, a year ago. I'm further confused. Is this the procedure that's followed for every student—to be punished a year later? What other infractions of student discipline can be delayed for a year? Or is this just for Marvonna?

I'd like to discuss this matter further. Please contact me at 555-212-1931 or via email ----

Thank you for giving this matter your attention,
Rosalita Baxter

In the vignette, the parent's email to the principal expresses her concern and frustration about an example of what can happen when communication and collaboration between educators and parents are minimal or *strained*. Rosalita is not the only parent with confusing experiences or having heard seemingly *impromptu*, inequitable rules with their children's school official. Families often assume everything is fine at school until there's notification that states otherwise. One of the most common problems is a lack of communication and engagement between parents or families and schools.

Our children and youth are surrounded by people to assist and support them throughout their educational journeys. Families, in all their forms across society, serve as the first teachers of their children. Schools become a place where children and youth socially interact on a regular basis, learning basic academic concepts and information in group settings.

Family and school are present across cultures, whether culture is expressed in terms of race, ethnicity, gender, socioeconomic position, language fluency, ability, sexual orientation, gender identity, or the many intersections that exist in society. Lindsey, Nuri-Robins, Terrell, & Lindsey (2018) observed that in every group, the family, as defined by culture, is the primary system of support in the education of children. In our schools, there's an opportunity for families and schools to lay a foundation of solid social, academic, and psychological skills for students.

Inclusive school leaders foster a partnering culture in which families, schools, and communities cultivate an environment that supports adults engaged in affective and effective relationship building, goal achievement, and equitable collaboration in support of students. Effective school leadership teams set the tone for appropriate behaviors on campus, which rules will be strictly enforced, and major activities to guide the school year. Strategic decisions are made regularly regarding how policies are to be implemented, how programs are to be assessed, how teachers are to be observed and evaluated, and how families and communities are to be engaged.

Educators, families, and community members acting in concert are critical to the success of students and schools. Parents want the best for their children: a safe, equitable, and caring environment. No matter the cultural composition of the school or school district; parents want the best for their children: a safe, equitable, and caring environment (O'Brien, 2017). The recent increase in school violence witnesses parents wanting to be more deeply engaged in consistent dialogue and decisions involving their children's safety, well-being, and learning at school.

This chapter introduces the rationale of why we, as educators, partner with or engage with families and community members. Given the prominent research that supports engagement as deep involvement and commitment to the community being served, it's important to recognize the various components of a culturally proficient engagement strategy. A Cultural Proficiency framework for community engagement is composed of carefully crafted and negotiated strategies undergirded with a moral imperative that guides our roles as educators to provide equitable access, opportunities, and outcomes for our students, families, and communities (Hawkins, 2016; Henderson & Mapp, 2002; Lindsey, Nuri-Robins, Terrell, & Lindsey, 2018; Mapp, 2018).

This chapter presents terms used to comprehensively explain family, school, and community partnerships that give rise to deeper levels of engagement in which all parties' roles and contributions are valued, respected, and utilized. Knowledge of terminology supports the development of a well-documented rationale on which to build foundations for cultural inclusiveness. The second section of this chapter discusses family, school, and community engagement studies which report that many families, particularly those diverse in color, socioeconomic status, and ability, have strained to be a part of their children's and youth's education, but often to no avail. Over the years, many families have faced a variety of challenges in being *meaningfully engaged*. Educators, too, have faced challenges related to family and community members' engagement. Creating school partnerships that encourage and influence families in becoming an integral part of students' educational lives and academic achievements is reported to be crucial, yet often unattainable. The final section of this chapter discusses the benefits for all of intentional inclusiveness and the shared responsibility of creating culturally proficient partnerships using the Framework and Tools of Cultural Proficiency.

CHANGING TIMES AND TERMINOLOGY

Over the years, various terms have been used to describe the parent-family-school relationship. In much the same way that schools and educational leadership have evolved, so too have the terms *parent and community involvement* and *parent and community engagement*. A variety of terms are used to express the relational partnership between and among participants who contribute to children's and youths' learning. Terms frequently used include *parent involvement, parent engagement, parent participation, family involvement, family engagement, home-school collaboration,* and *family-school partnership.*

Parent involvement emphasizes the caregivers (e.g., parents, grandparents, step-parents, foster parents). In EdSource's *The Power of Parents: Research Underscores the Impact of Parent Involvement in Schools* (2014a), parent involvement is defined as "the efforts a school district makes to seek parent input in making decisions for the school district and each individual school site . . ." (p. 3). In her explanation of the distinction between parent involvement and family engagement, Dr. Debbie Pushor, professor in the Department of Curriculum Studies at the University of Saskatchewan, recently defined the difference between the two terms. "With parent involvement, parents are expected to serve the school's agenda. Parent engagement, in contrast, honours parents' place & voice in their child's teaching, learning & development - at home as well as at school. Two different concepts!" (November 27, 2018, 7:20 p.m., Tweet). More recently, changing *parent* to the word *family* denotes an expansion that demonstrates there is often more than one or two persons involved in the child's or youth's learning and education (California Department of Education, 2014; US Department of Education, 2016). From the wellspring of terminology, we focus on the following words:

Family engagement is described by The National Family, School and Community Engagement Working Group as the support that families provide their children to "achieve more effective educational opportunities" (NFSCEWG; 2009). In 2018, the Global Research Project *"defined . . . family engagement as moving from where we are now—a scattered, marginal, and unaligned set of programs and policies—to more strategic and systemic approaches to family and community engagement in and out of school and from birth through young adulthood"* (Global Family Research Foundation, 2018, p. 4). The National Association for Family, School, and Community Engagement (NAFSCE; 2009) adopted the following as crucial elements of family engagement:

1. Family engagement is a shared responsibility in which schools and other community agencies and organizations are committed to reaching out to engage families in meaningful ways and in which families are committed to actively supporting their children's learning and development.

2. Family engagement is continuous across a child's life and entails enduring commitment, but changing parent roles as children mature into young adulthood.

3. Effective family engagement cuts across and reinforces learning in the multiple settings where children learn—at home, in prekindergarten programs, in schools, in after school programs, in faith-based institutions, and in the community (https://nafsce.org/page/definition).

Community engagement includes the many varied groups of people within children's and the school's circle of influence. According to the Reform Support

Network (2014), sponsored by the US Department of Education, community engagement's purpose is

> to ensure that school improvement is done with the community, not to the community. It recognizes how integral schools are to their communities, and how much parents and communities have to offer as partners when fundamental change must occur in schools. A school exists to educate the children of a community, and by embracing community engagement, political and educational leaders demonstrate their recognition that families and communities have an important say in what happens inside its doors. (p. 3)

Communities help define the values in the neighborhood and the culture of the surrounding areas. Businesses, religious institutions, government agencies, and higher educational institutions within the community impact and influence schools, which in turn impact students. We further recognize that school personnel within the school setting influence and impact students' learning, achievement, and well-being.

School and educator describe any representative of the PreK-12 educational institution such as the teacher, principal, counselor, coach, secretary, aide, or custodian. Clarification and use of these terms will help us establish that anyone at the school, near the school geographically, or even anyone connected with the school or the student can help in serving as a partner or in arranging partnerships.

Community partnership illustrates the long-term commitment to building relationships among families, schools, and communities. Partnering allows all involved the opportunities to contribute, invest, and benefit from students' academic, social, and emotional achievements. With children and youth as the focal point of attention, families, schools, and their communities combine to serve as the context for supporting and engaging partnerships.

INFORMED BY RELATED STUDIES: FROM STRAIN TO INCLUSION

In our review of the literature on family, school, and community engagement, we had several interesting findings. There have been studies to reveal parent and educator perspectives about one another and their respective roles, efficacy, opportunities, and parent effectiveness (Foster, Young, & Young, 2017; Gettinger & Guetschow, 1998; Leadership Conference Education Fund, 2017). More recent studies, though, have honored parents' and families' voices by simply asking them questions. In our experience, simply asking families what, if any, concerns they might hold about their schools, what they really want from schools, and how they want to engage with schools provides a strong starting point for partnering and, ultimately, engagement with schools (Henderson & Mapp, 2002).

WHAT PARENTS WANT TO KNOW AND WHAT
PARENTS WANT EDUCATORS TO KNOW

A 2017 Rice University study of family and community engagement surveyed 7,200 public school parents (DeNisco, 2018). Results displayed in Table 2.1 indicated only 34 percent of public school parents were *very satisfied* with family and community engagement, in marked contrast to private school parents (50 percent) and charter school parents (47 percent). Parents rated family and community engagement as the most important factor of satisfaction with their child's school. In terms of community engagement, 46 percent of parents reported *satisfaction* with school communication; 45 percent reported parent-teacher conferences suited their schedules; and 44 percent stated the school clearly explains how their child is graded. The study also noted parents reported that districts frequently fail to offer them a voice in the education system. Professor Vikas Mittal, the study's lead researcher, remarks:

> When we talk to principals and administrators, some of them say, "Parents just want a lot of extracurriculars," or "Parents just want good teachers." What we found is that the biggest weight that parents give is actually to family and community engagement. (n.p.)

TABLE 2.1
Family and Community Engagement Satisfaction Results

Parents who are *very satisfied* with family and community engagement:
Public school parents: 34%
Private school parents: 50%
Charter school parents: 47%
When it comes to specific measures of engagement:
46% of parents report satisfaction with school communication
45% of parents say parent-teacher conferences suit their schedules
44% of parents say the school clearly explains how their child is graded

Source: Collaborative for Customer-Based Execution and Strategy Benchmark K–12 School Study, Rice University, 2017

The first major statewide California School Parent Survey ($N = 15,829$) examined "parental perceptions of climate, school problems, and school encouragement of parental involvement" (Berkowitz et al., 2017, p. 1). The findings indicate and support past research (Henderson & Mapp, 2002) that school efforts to welcome parents and families are a crucial step. Considering parents' and families' cultural and social capital and backgrounds was viewed as important and key to increasing engagement (Berkowitz et al., 2017; Mapp, 2018).

How often have we heard the phrase "parents don't care," or "*they* don't want to be involved"? Unfortunately, statements such as these are too often sprinkled in conversations educators have with one another. Similarly, we have heard parents make comments such as "teachers don't care" or "they just don't like [name of child]."

We believe that families, schools, and communities care and want the best for their children, notwithstanding the tenor and tone of the comments shared above. We also believe that teachers, who are the vast majority of educators, care about the academic, social, and psychological well-being of students and want family and community participation and support and involvement within schools.

Two recent national polls on schools and schooling provide glimpses into what parents want from schools and how they want to be involved: *What Parents Want From Public Schools?* (O'Brien, 2017), based on a poll conducted by The American Federation of Teachers (Winter 2017–2018), and the New Education Majority Poll: *Black and Latino Parents and Families on Education and Their Children's Future* (Leadership Conference Education Fund, May 2017) by Phi Delta Kappa's Leadership Education Conference.

In the first poll, *What Parents Want From Public Schools?*, 1,200 parents stated what their concerns were about schools. Their biggest concerns were about inadequate funding for schools and too much attention on testing. According to this study, budget cuts were unfavorable and impacted the school's role in students' preparation for life. The second poll's results reported that inequities in school funding was a priority concern, particularly for Black and Latinx families and communities. "Ninety percent of African American and 57 percent of Latino adult family members believe schools in their communities do not receive the same amount of funding as schools in white communities" (O'Brien, 2017, n.p.). DeWitt (2018) provided a deeper examination of parental views of schools and schooling. In surveying over 7,000 parents, DeWitt reported that only 29 percent felt they had a voice in their child's education. These parents felt their voices weren't valued for input into curriculum and policy and that administrators didn't engage and respect their opinions.

Reflection

What concerns are voiced by family members at your school? In what ways do family members voice their concerns? Please use the space below to record your responses.

_____

_____

_____

_____

In their study with African American parents, Louque and Latunde (2014) discuss that sometimes schools and families have a *strained relationship*. Mapp (2003) posited that the *strain* emanates from several different sources. A strained relationship could stem from being made to feel unwelcome, inadequate, or even less capable (California Department of Education, 2014; Faber, 2015; Weyer, 2015). Often a source of strain is from the parent or family member's own negative childhood school experiences. Faber (2015) expressed that part of the problem in making stronger connections with families is because some parents and families have had unpleasant school experiences themselves and that teachers often look at parents from a deficit lens. He goes on to say that what educators are essentially telling parents and families is, "You don't know something and we do, and we're going to ask you to come into school, a place where you don't feel comfortable, and we are going to tell you what you don't know. And then, we (the staff) are going to stand around and wonder why you don't show up, and we're just going to repeat that cycle over and over again" (p. 2). Awareness of this sometimes uncomfortable feeling that families and communities report having felt marginalized leads the culturally inclusive educator to reach out to family and community members in nonthreatening, non-condescending ways.

Our challenge as inclusive educators is to ease the strain and decrease the levels of discomfort. It is our responsibility to ensure a welcome tone in our schools and classrooms prevails over traces of mistrust. Ascertaining what families and communities want or need and what educators want or need is a seemingly safe place to start.

Not surprisingly, Epstein (2011) found that families want to engage in activities they believe will help their children achieve academically. We say *not surprisingly* due to our experiences that often we encounter educators seemingly surprised when discovering family and community members are more alike across cultural groups than ways in which they differ. Families want to engage in ways that make sense to them.

Families have clearly voiced that they really do want to know about their children's education. Weaver (2017) describes families' interests in knowing if their child has been absent, not turning in homework, or misbehaving. Families don't want to learn of their child's misdeeds at back-to-school night. Essentially, parents want consistent and ongoing communication. Families want to be informed about major school activities and events and they want to know that their opinions are heard and respected and that their voices matter (Berkowitz et al., 2017).

Reflection

When you hear phrases such as *parents don't care* or *teachers don't care about the students,* how do you respond to those phrases? In what ways are you willing to examine your assumptions about parents? If you have a new colleague at your school, what would you want them to know about the parents, families, and community served by your school? Please use the space below to record your responses.

_____

_____

_____

_____

BENEFITS OF PARTNERING FOR ALL

Creating and maintaining family, school, and community partnerships is ever important in our increasingly diverse society. Partnerships greatly impact communities and society at large because of benefits produced. Researchers may not always agree with the definition of family engagement, but they most often agree that there are great benefits family–school engagement provides (Allen, 2007; Boonk, Gijselaers, Ritzen, & Brand-Gruwel, 2018; Constantino, 2003; Epstein et al., 2002; Henderson, 2016). When all constituents interact positively for the benefit of the child's education, the family, school, and community benefit. For families, engagement demonstrates confidence and trust in the school's ability to educate their children. This provides a sense of fulfillment in remaining involved in their children's education and learning. For students, benefits of parent and family engagement have been shown to reduce absenteeism and improve student achievement. Not only do benefits manifest in the academic realm of learning, but students' social skills and positive behaviors improve. For students, partnering means higher educational, academic, and social-psychological success. Students' attitude toward school and learning has been shown to be more positive. For schools, higher levels of participation increase parents' volunteer time in school-related activities. School image is improved throughout the community, and families have more satisfaction with the school. For communities, it means having an influence on present and future members, as well as the community environment as a whole. It also creates opportunities for increased interactions and participations for businesses, churches, and community projects. For educators and schools, this means they are an integrated part of providing the best to schools and society (Epstein, Coates, Simon, & Salinas, 1997; Henderson & Mapp, 2002). Educational benefits have been identified as to why school, family, and community engagement and partnerships support the academic achievement and social-emotional development of students and all community partners. With these kinds of odds, no wonder families, schools, and communities strive to be engaged. The benefits of family, school, and community engagement are seen as a win-win for all.

Reflection

What might be some specific benefits you see for students attending your school or schools in your district? Please use the space below to record your response.

_____

_____

_____

_____

FAMILY AND COMMUNITY ENGAGEMENT AND
LINK TO STUDENT ACHIEVEMENT

Increased student academic achievement as a primary purpose of families, schools, and communities developing partnerships and engagement with each other has been well documented (Dantas & Manyack, 2010; Epstein & Dauber, 1991; Lezotte, 1997; Quezada, Alexandrowicz, & Molina, 2015). Evidence suggests that when families, schools, and communities develop partnerships, student academic achievement increases and greater participation by families is evident.

Studies by the Global Family Research Foundation (2018) and others (Hoover-Dempsey, 1987) indicate family and community engagement being central to promoting student academic achievement and for engagement being one of the strongest predictors of student success, well-being, and overall development. Their works confirm that "the achievement gap between lower- and higher-income students is largely tied to an 'opportunity gap'—differences in families' ability to access learning and enrichment experiences both in and out of school" (International Classification of Functioning, 2001, p. 1).

When schools, families, community, government, faith-based organizations, and businesses work in partnership, they all contribute to the general climate of schools as well as to student academic achievement. Villani (1999) and Epstein (2011) join this chorus of voices in sensing the need for engaging families in their children's education in and out of schools. Epstein also says loudly and authoritatively that schools and communities can no longer ignore the diverse communities served by our schools. It is our responsibility to have five sectors—schools, families, community, government, and businesses—join together to share in the responsibility to develop culturally proficient educators and a mutual cooperation and trust for our children and youth.

Community engagement is not limited to our PreK–12 schools. Community engagement extends to institutions of higher education as well. It is incumbent on our colleges of education to ensure their educator preparation programs integrate the inclusivity and equity tenets of Cultural Proficiency with regard to family, school, and community engagement and partnerships in the curricula of all teacher, counselor, and administrator preparation programs. The same holds true for school district staff development and professional learning programs. Engaging students' and their communities' cultures as assets when interacting with families and cultural communities is at the core of inclusive family, school, and community engagement practices.

CULTURALLY PROFICIENT LEADERSHIP
AND ENGAGEMENT

Much has been written on school leadership and how school leaders impact various aspects of school including the school environment, how policies are developed, how discipline practices are implemented, and how communication is exchanged

(Riehl, 2000). Family and community engagement can be posed as an *old* situation with *new* solutions. With all that school leaders are responsible for doing, how do they create partnerships beneficial to the achievement of students as well as create positive school climates? How can school leaders increase parent participation and focus on family engagement, achievement, and school success? Culturally proficient school leaders partner with families and communities purposefully. Leaders who have a value for partnering as a crucial part of the learning experience for students by definition value the cultural capital families and communities bring to the school community.

A MORAL IMPERATIVE AND SHARED RESPONSIBILITY FOR CREATING CULTURALLY PROFICIENT ENGAGEMENT

Inclusive education embraced as a moral imperative has school leaders who view a function of their role to be bridging communication between the school community and the diverse communities served by the school or district. Culturally proficient school leaders proactively reach out to the various cultures served by the school and help their colleagues recognize, honor, and embrace the funds of knowledge and the cultural capital of each cultural group that composes the community served by the school.

Fullan (2003) describes moral imperative in terms of the role of a school leader being a helper to faculty and staff. The leader's role is to help others see new opportunities and possibilities in *old* situations. Leaders who view situations that involve issues arising from equity and diversity with an inclusive perspective and purpose have a stronger emotional connection to the school community. With an inclusive perspective, school leaders are more apt to embrace cultural diversity as asset-based and engage with their diverse communities in meaningful ways. The Tools of Cultural Proficiency (Chapter 1) serve as a lens for framing individual and systemic actions in service of the diverse communities within your schools and districts.

Educationally, partnerships provide social and relational aspects of education. The relationship between schools and student success and family and community engagement is interdependent to not only support one another, but to encourage and visibly and verbally affirm. The exclusion and isolation frequently experienced by diverse families in US schools, particularly those who are African American, Latinx, and from communities of poverty may act as barriers to optimal family engagement in education and contribute to student issues of inequity.

In acknowledging the assets that families bring to partnering, funds of knowledge and cultural capital render deficit models inconsequential. Embracing cultural assets serves "to alter perceptions of working-class or poor communities and to view these households primarily in terms of their strengths and resources (or funds of knowledge)" (González, Moll, & Amanti, 2005, p. x). Knowing and trusting that parents have accumulated funds of knowledge to survive circumstances, navigate systems, and adjust in everyday settings demonstrates educators' strength of character.

Bourdieu (1986) describes cultural capital as knowledge, education, and social skills acquired over time. Cultural capital exists within us. We bring cultural capital with us when we go to school as do families when they arrive at schools. Families provide social constructs in their homes for their children at an early age, therefore providing already established *capital*. Families' cultural capital is to be valued and respected in order to diminish social divisions and inequality (Louque & Latunde, 2014). Culturally proficient educators who recognize funds of knowledge and cultural capital as positive and as contributions to school climate are bound to see and experience growth in participation of families and an increase in student connectedness with their schools and educational experiences (Allen, 2007; González et al., 2005).

The Essential Elements of Cultural Competence/Proficiency foster learning about families' funds of knowledge and cultural capital and how embracing them as assets positively impacts families' perspectives of partnering. Culturally proficient family and community engagement, as reflected in Figure 2.1, opens doors for everyone to have access to educational opportunities and learning outcomes. The Cultural Proficiency Framework provides tools for educators to use in identifying educational inequities and developing and implementing equitable and inclusive actions.

FIGURE 2.1

Be Intentional: Equity and Inclusion

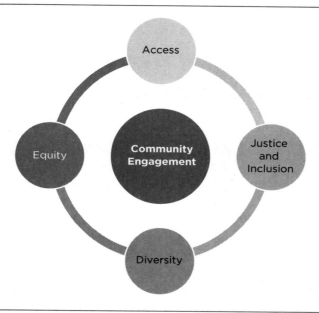

Are families at your school valued? What indicators might you have that families are or are not valued? How are families' funds of knowledge demonstrated in your school or district? Please use the space below to record your responses.

_____

_____

_____

_____

The importance of family and community engagement cannot be overemphasized. From birth through adolescence and beyond, families play important roles in their children's learning and development. For students from cultural groups historically marginalized in schools to be successful, family engagement must be proactively sought and conducted as shared responsibility by educators and family/community members. Shared responsibilities are evident where families and schools come together to embrace student-centered learning supported by strong instructional systems and focused leadership, to host strong professional development for teachers, and to engage community and business partners. The intent is for the partnerships to develop family engagement pathways that will start early and evolve over time by taking into consideration students' age and maturation context development. Such pathways take into account multiple settings such as schools, homes, and community spaces, as well as libraries, museums, afterschool programs, faith-based organizations, and higher education institutions.

OUR _WHY_

Culturally proficient approaches to family engagement describe all levels of interaction among and between parents, families, schools, and the students served by the school.

Schools include educators and staff, business and academic functions of schooling, as well as the range of curricular and co-curricular functions needed to support student learning. Family and community engagement occurs when relationships are valued and action related, not superficially and tacitly involved. Building such partnerships is the foundation for supporting student success. The chapters that follow present specific avenues by which families, schools, and communities can be engaged, as well as lessons learned from the authors' personal and professional experiences in building culturally proficient partnerships.

Therefore, this book's purpose is threefold. First, to promote equitable family, school, and community engagement practices grounded in the Cultural Proficiency

Framework. Second, to increase interest in and development of effective family, school, and community engagement relationship building and partnering actions. Third, to give voice to all who want to make partnerships and engagement integral parts of all students' schooling experiences.

We want for you to create and develop your capacity to recruit and welcome family and community members into the daily lives of schools and schooling. We encourage you to work with the diverse communities in your school or community to promote *continuous engagement* through equitable and inclusive policies, practices, and educator actions that lead to student academic and social success. Earlier in this chapter, we described research and related literature to support the reality that students achieve and do better in school when families and community members are engaged in the students' education.

Reflection

Going Deeper Reflection

How might you describe your commitment to family and community engagement? In what ways do you describe your school or district's commitment to family and community engagement? What questions arise for you about yourself and your school or district?

_____

_____

_____

_____

Going Deeper Dialogic Questions

In what ways might you engage your colleagues in learning about family and community engagement benefits and practices? What might be your school or district's assets or challenges in terms of family and community engagement? What might be some of the challenges facing your school or district in terms of family and community engagement?

_____

_____

_____

_____

SUMMARY

Forming strong collaborations among families, communities, and schools has long been known to be advantageous for students. Providing opportunities for access, creating equitable policies, and facilitating learning for and with diverse family and community members promotes an atmosphere of cultural awareness and continuous engagement.

LOOKING AHEAD: CHAPTER 3

Chapter 3 begins with a brief historical overview for understanding current legal mandates and educational standards. Review and quick study of the historical timeline provides understanding of the moral imperative for purposeful actions to increase the importance of partnering in education. Next mentioned are legal reasons why family, school, and community collaborations are interconnected for the benefit of students and, finally, that as educational leaders, we have professional standards that serve as guidelines for developing inclusive actions.

I speak not for myself but for those without voice . . . those who have fought for their rights . . . their right to live in peace, their right to be treated with dignity, their right to equality of opportunity, their right to be educated.

—MALALA YOUSAFZAI, 2016, P. 16

The previous chapter highlighted benefits that focused on families, schools, students, and their communities. This chapter underscores the importance of family and community engagement by identifying and investigating the historical, legal, and educational bases for creating and maintaining inclusive family, school, and community partnerships. The historical overview presented herein briefly explains the historical, legal, and educational shifts that have occurred and that continue to evolve in the United States. Legal mandates, combined with educational considerations, have given rise to guidelines that form the foundation for purposeful commitments and actions focused on the importance of family, school, and community partnering in service of our children, youth, and adult learners. The legal and educational responsibilities of family and community engagement honor the complexities and commonalities of contemporary PreK–12 schooling that involves families in a child's schooling experience.

FAMILY, SCHOOL, AND COMMUNITY ENGAGEMENT HAS EVOLVED OVER TIME

Hiatt-Michael (1994), in her seminal literature review of parent involvement, found that parent involvement has evolved throughout history, often riding on religious, social, and/or political waves. In the original eighteenth century colonies, schools and their education programs were created and controlled by religious leaders within local townships. School boards served to oversee the administration of schools. Curricula were composed of prescribed religious studies, reading, and writing. Parental lay school boards' philosophies reflected the religious beliefs of the founding community members.

The National Congress of Mothers (NCM) was formed in 1897 to address many education issues members believed were not being addressed by schools. Most were middle-income parents aware of the educational system and how it worked. They promoted kindergarten as well as health education and began to coalesce as national, state, and local units. NCM gave rise to the Parent-Teacher Association (PTA) that has proliferated across the country and serves to support community-school communication and problem-solving functions.

TWENTIETH CENTURY AND BEYOND

Early in the twentieth century, schools evolved in local communities and tended to reflect the social classes as well as the racial and ethnic profiles of their local constituents. In the post–World War II United States, schools continued to change and evolve to meet the needs of a rapidly industrializing and growing economy. Populations were expanding and people were migrating to growing suburban communities. As school populations were growing, becoming more mobile, and becoming more diverse, PreK–12 schools and higher educational institutions expanded and were seen as the knowledge spaces that addressed the educational needs of both children and adults. By the late twentieth century, concerns about schools and educational quality were being raised by parents, politicians, members of the business community, and educators across local, state, and national constituencies.

Early national reports to address family, school, and community engagement include the Coleman Report (1966) which, among other findings, labeled family background characteristics as reasons for disparate academic achievements of ethnic minority students and is too often used to inform deficit-based approaches in working with low income and with historically marginalized communities of racial and ethnic students of color. Later, *A Nation at Risk* (National Commission on Excellence in Education, 1983) supported the need to connect families with children's school experiences if we were to close academic achievement disparities. Collectively, these reports focused on cultural deficit models centered on disparate achievement of students from low-income communities due to impoverished language environment in the home.

Cultural-deficit models and approaches informed many of the educational reforms intended to support family, school, and community engagement programs supported by the federal government. Chapter 1 (later Title 1) of the Elementary and Secondary Education Act (ESEA) as well as Head Start during the 1960s and 1970s, and authorized student-support services to include families, were often built around deficit-based approaches. The effect of deficit-based approaches is embodied in educator beliefs and school policies centered on correcting what is wrong in students' cultures in order for students to be academically successful.

The period from the 1980s through the first decade after 2000 witnessed the emergence of federal policies and guidelines to mandate parents' involvement in education decisions that affected their children. Recognition that schools and the communities they served were complex systems provided policy makers the impetus to develop educational guidelines intended to be inclusive and at the same time address lingering accountability concerns. Accountability issues included concerns about effective use of federal resources and concerns over persistent access and academic achievement gaps. Though an argument can be made about effectiveness, concerns about levels of parent and community involvement were being addressed along with concerns over narrowing and closing *achievement gaps*. Deficit approaches were beginning to ebb as educational leaders were being held accountable to authentic parent and community engagement. In truth, definitions and illustrations of participation, involvement, and engagement were dependent on local interpretations.

In 2002, the No Child Left Behind Act (NCLB) was negotiated across political lines to address lingering concerns with equitable educational opportunities and outcomes and focused on five areas: (1) local educational agency policy, (2) school parental involvement policy, (3) policy involvement, (4) shared responsibility for high student performance, and (5) building capacity for involvement (NCLB, 2002). NCLB required local education agencies to write policies outlining expectations for parental involvement. The implementation of policy as well as program evaluation was left to the discretion of the local educational agency (LEA). This policy further amended the Individuals with Disabilities Education Act (IDEA; 2004) in that it maintained the importance of family engagement and participation in special education at all school grade levels. IDEA policy is one of the most effectively implemented and successful federal policies for the integration and incorporation of school and family engagement in children's education. It seemed for a time that one's socioeconomic neighborhood may not dictate the quality of educational experience. However, as too often is the case with twentieth century educational policies and reforms focused on addressing equitable educational issues, the promise of NCLB outstripped the realities of implementation. That said, a legacy of NCLB may be that sociocultural educational achievement gaps became part of the public discourse, and the involvement of parent and community members in educational decision making was becoming more representative of local communities.

On December 10, 2015, President Obama signed the most recent authorization of the Elementary and Secondary Act (ESEA) known as Every Student Succeeds Act (ESSA) effectively sunsetting NCLB and ushering in mechanisms for deeper engagement of family and community members in educational decision making. Anne Henderson from the Annenberg Institute for School Reform (2016) highlighted new items added to ESSA in her "Quick Brief" to Family Engagement for Title I Parent and Family Engagement:

- Replacing *parent involvement* with *family engagement*.

- Funding tied to school districts conducting effective outreach to all parents.

- Providing written policies to parents and family members establishing expectations and objectives for meaningful parent and family engagement.

- Having written and available policies for collaborating with employers, business school leaders, philanthropic organizations, or individuals who have expertise in engaging parents and family members in education, and involving parents on advisory board member committees reflecting the demographic makeup of the community.

- Dedicating at least 1 percent of Title I allocation to assisting school districts with carrying out family engagement activities consistent with districts' parent and family engagement policy. Activities include *professional development* for teachers, parents, administrators, and the community at large; *home-based* programs that will reach parents and family members;

disseminating information of best practices on family engagement in particular with economically disadvantaged parents and family members; collaborating with community-based organizations through funding schools to collaborate with organizations or employers with a track record of success in improving and increasing parent and family engagement; and *other activities* that can support activities and strategies to support parent and family engagement based on the parent and family engagement policy (Henderson, 2016).

Another key mandate of ESSA "focused on early childhood home visitation, leading to the creation of the 2012 Maternal, Infant, and Early Childhood Home Visiting Act, which set aside federal funds so states could establish home visitation programs for low-income and immigrant families" (Global Family Research Foundation 2018, p. 6; Patient Protection and Affordable Care Act, 2010).

Reflection

Thinking of your school or district, in what ways do you describe family or community engagement? How might you describe this engagement from a historical perspective? What was the impetus for including or not including families? Please use the space below to record your response.

_____

_____

_____

_____

FEDERAL AND STATE COURT DECISIONS AND LEGISLATIVE ACTIONS THAT FOSTER FAMILY, SCHOOL, AND COMMUNITY PARTNERSHIPS

Legal supports for family, school, and community collaboration are interconnected with historical shifts in educational practices and school policies. Federal and state court decisions and legislative actions beginning in the mid-twentieth century have addressed educational inequities. The landmark 1954 United States Supreme Court decision, *Brown v. Board of Education of Topeka*, found that separate but equal schooling did not provide Black children with the same education provided to White children. The *Brown* decision was preceded in California by the *Alvarez v. Lemon Grove* (1931) and the *Mendez v. Westminster* (1947) State Supreme Court decisions that addressed the discriminatory policies and practices of providing separate schools for Mexican American students and contributed to the slow national push for desegregation of schools. With the *Serrano v. Priest* (1971) decision, the US Supreme Court effectively reorganized state funding with attention to leveling funding among well- and under-resourced school districts. Under the leadership of the US Congress and the signature of President Ford, Pub. L. No. 94-142 (1975) mandated equitable school services be provided to children with special needs. In *Lau v. Nichols* (1974), the US Supreme Court found in support of Chinese parents in San Francisco that their children be taught in a manner that students would understand leading to the development of bilingual education programs.

The Every Student Succeeds Act (ESSA), signed into law in 2015, is the most recent Elementary and Secondary Act (ESEA) authorization. This law allows the fifty states to lead in developing and implementing their education policy plans and goals. Additionally, the law provides fiscal resources for under-resourced schools through giving schools and districts increased flexibility and freedom in creating their own education plans and related funding formulas (Klein, 2015; Ujifusa, 2016). Family and community engagement provisions are instrumental requirements of ESSA.

In this era and context of increased flexibility in applying federal and state guidelines, it is important to recognize family and community engagement for what it is and how it is represented in different settings. As an illustration, in 2013, the California legislature and governor signed AB 97, a Local Control Funding Formula (LCFF), as a sweeping bill designed to reform its school funding system. To comply with the LCFF, district leaders were instructed to collaborate with stakeholders (e.g., parents, students, faculty, staff) to adopt a Local Control and Accountability Plan (LCAP). LCAPs must address eight state priority areas: (1) student achievement, (2) student engagement, (3) school climate, (4) parental involvement, (5) course access, (6) implementation of the Common Core Standards, (7) basic services, and (8) other student outcomes. As of 2015, twenty states had incorporated family engagement prekindergarten programs and fifteen additional states are considering implementing similar programs (California Department of Education, 2014; Weyer, 2015).

When local school and district leaders embrace legislation that supports, promotes, and in many cases mandates family engagement in PreK–12 schools, our children, youth, and communities benefit. Federal and state guidelines can be embraced as mere mechanisms of compliance or, in the case of family, school, and community engagement, can be viewed as an opportunity to embrace, design, and implement as a moral imperative. Inclusive engagement policies and practices focused on the students who attend their schools, not the students from a previous generation or the students that some "wish they could have." The choice is ours. The responsibility is ours, too, and must not be squandered if we are truly serious about inclusive approaches to family, school, and community engagement.

EDUCATIONAL RATIONALE FOR FAMILY, SCHOOL, AND COMMUNITY ENGAGEMENT

Educationally, we are charged by professional standards to engage families and communities. The National Policy Board for Educational Administration

(2015) seeks to develop foundational principles of educational leadership. The Professional Standards for Educational Leaders guides development of leadership programs for beginning administrators and experienced school leaders. Through the efforts to ensure policies and leadership program expectancies, the standards emphasize family and community engagement for all educational leaders. Standard 8, for example, focuses on meaningful engagement of families and communities:

Standard 8. Meaningful Engagement of Families and Communities.
Effective educational leaders engage families and the community in meaningful, reciprocal, and mutually beneficial ways to promote each student's academic success and well-being.

More specifically for teachers, the National Board for Professional Teaching Standards (2016) advocates that "accomplished teachers communicate regularly with students' parents and guardians. Teachers inform them about their children's accomplishments and challenges, responding to their questions, listening to their concerns and respecting their views" (p. 37). Here are a few examples of state professional standards for education leaders and teachers that encourage a culture and school environment of engaging families and communities:

- **California's Professional Standards for Education Leaders (2014)**

  Standard 4: *Family and Community Engagement. Education leaders collaborate with families and other stakeholders to address diverse student and community interests and mobilize community resources (Commission on Teacher Credentialing, 2014).*

- **New York State Teaching Standards (2011)**

  Standard VI: *Professional Responsibilities and Collaboration*

  Element VI.2: *Teachers engage and collaborate with colleagues and the community to develop and sustain a common culture that supports high expectations for student learning.*

  Element VI.3: *Teachers communicate and collaborate with families, guardians, and caregivers to enhance student development and success.*

- **Tennessee Professional Teaching Standard (n.d.)**

  Standard 10: *Colleagues, Parents, and Community. Candidates foster relationships with school colleagues, parents, and agencies in the larger community to support student's learning and well-being.*

These and other professional standards commission educational leaders to welcome families, create positive and collaborative relationships, and value the community's resources to promote student learning. These examples further demonstrate the importance to pursue collaborative relationships with families for the purpose of enhancing student learning and achievement.

IMPORTANCE OF EDUCATIONAL RESEARCH IN BUILDING FAMILY, SCHOOL, AND COMMUNITY ENGAGEMENT IN DIVERSE COMMUNITIES

Asset-based approaches to families and communities embrace culture, language, and socioeconomic status as foundations on which to build school-community partnerships. Family engagement is most effective when families, schools, educators, and communities mutually plan and assess programs, strategies, and desired student outcomes. To co-create effective family, school, and community engagement and partnerships might require educators to engage a shift in thinking and behavior from a mindset of viewing cultural groups as *other*, thus shifting from being incapable of effective management to a mindset of being able to discern and value the assets inherent in cultural groups. An asset-based approach functions as a means by which to structure engagement. Shifting mindsets of educators can lead to systemic changes of school policies and a broader public understanding of effective family engagement practices in the diverse and varied cultural communities served by the school or district (Dantas & Manyak, 2010; Epstein 2015).

The year 2014 marked the first time in the modern era when the United States' PreK–12 student population did not have a majority group (National Center for Educational Statistics, 2014). A little over 50 (50.3) percent of our nation's student population identified as Black, Hispanic, Asian, Native Hawaiian, Pacific Islander, American Indian/Alaska Native, or other non-White groups. All other students (49.7 percent) identified as White. Not only are the majority of students diverse, their parents and family members are as well. In twenty-one states, including California, a minimum of 50 percent of all students are eligible for free and reduced lunch (Southern Education Foundation, 2017), which means that there is racial/ethnic diversity and socioeconomic diversity as well. In this age of increasing diversity, technology, instant information, and *fake news*, educators need to know how to navigate issues related to social justice, diversity, and culture with parents, families, communities, and students in the nation's schools (Hawkins, 2016).

This section is written to address specific groups of families who represent diverse economic and cultural backgrounds. Studies regarding these groups continually demonstrate increased academic, social, and emotional skills as well. So how can we close the "opportunity gap" so our children and their families may flourish? For further references and resources, here are some annotated bibliographies:

- Harvard Family Research Project (2012). *Family engagement and children with disabilities: A resource guide for educators and parents.*
  - This guide presents a selected list of resources that can help families with practical suggestions and strategic advice on advocacy and navigation through the various different education processes such as due process, assessment and intervention, student learning, and partnering with schools.
- Quezada, Reyes L., Alexandrowicz, Viviana, & Molina, Sarina (Eds.) (2015). *Family, school community engagement and partnerships: An imperative for K–12, and colleges of education in the development of 21st century educators.* UK: Routledge.

- Their review of related studies about family, school, and community engagement and partnerships reinforced the notion that when schools, families, and community groups work as partners to support learning, children tend to do better in school, stay in school longer, and like school more.

- The Leadership Conference Education Fund (2017). The 2nd Annual New Education Majority Poll (May 2017). *Black and Latino parents and families on education and their children's future.* The Leadership Conference Education Fund. The Leadership Conference on Civil and Human Rights.
  - Findings from 600 Black and 600 Latinx families of their aspirations, beliefs, and children's education and the school systems. Racial disparity, inequity, and unfairness were key to their concerns, particularly with funding and school quality. Parents and families sensed that in schools where their child's teachers are mostly White the schools were *not really trying* to educate their children compared to schools with mostly Black or mostly Latinx teachers.

- Thompson, Gail (2003). *What African American parents want educators to know.* Westport, CT: Greenwood Publishing.
  - The results of a purposive, nonrandom sample of 129 African American parents and families are presented regarding academics, learning, discipline at school, and beliefs about teachers. As reported by the families, one of the highest variables correlating to children's attitude about school is frequent encounters with racism.

- Weiss, Heather B., Bouffard, Suzanne M., Bridglall, Beatrice L., & Gordon, Edmund W. (2009) and *Reframing family involvement in education: Supporting families to support educational equity.* Teachers College, Columbia University.
  - This report argues for research-based progress on family involvement to be co-created by scholars, practitioners, entrepreneurs, and families. In order to achieve educational equity and close achievement and opportunity gaps, a more integrated platform of new policies and legislation is required.

- Zarate, Maria (2007). *Understanding Latino parental involvement in education: Perceptions, expectations, and recommendation.* Tomas Rivera Policy Institute, University of Southern California.
  - Researchers examined four varying areas: (1) Latinx parent perceptions of their participation in the education of their children; (2) Teacher expectations of parental involvement; (3) Programmatic initiatives of addressing parental involvement in education; and (4) Latinx students' perceptions of the role of parental involvement in their education.

Reflection

Going Deeper Reflection

As you consider your school, school district, and the culturally and linguistically diverse families you serve, what questions do you have with regard to family, school, and community engagement and partnerships? What new questions does this chapter raise for you?

_____

_____

_____

_____

Going Deeper Dialogic Questions

Using your professional learning mechanism such as Professional Learning Community or Grade Level or Department meetings, how would you describe the levels of family and community engagement in your school? To what extent are there consistencies or inconsistencies among grade levels or department units? What questions are surfacing for you? What might be the next steps for you or your school to consider? What burning question(s) might you want to pose to your colleagues?

_____

_____

_____

_____

SUMMARY

This chapter presented an overview of historical, legal, and educational considerations that bring family, school, and community engagement to the forefront of school leaders' obligations. Culturally proficient leaders must keep family, school, and community engagement a priority because of the strong connection partnerships bring to student achievement. Three research-based theories laid the foundation for this book's guide for school leaders and educational policy.

LOOKING AHEAD: CHAPTER 4

If one looks at the opportunities of family, school, and community engagement in terms of building blocks, Chapter 2 guides educators to know the benefits of parent, family, and community engagement. Chapter 3 adds the building blocks of learning the moral imperative of effective engagement is rooted in historical, legal, and educational forces that have fostered equity and inclusion. In Chapter 4, you will learn about the historical connections and models of Epstein, Constantino, and Mapp and Kuttner regarding family, school, and community engagement. Their contributions to the realities of engagement and partnering have evolved in a manner to provide educators with a framework for developing and maintaining inclusive and equitable parent, family, and community engagement practices.

PART II

Embracing to Engage

4

How Cultural Proficiency Intersects With Family Engagement

Almost as color defines vision itself, race shapes the cultural eye – what we do and do not notice, the reach of empathy and the alignment of response.

This subliminal force recommends care in choosing a point of view for a history grounded in race.

—TAYLOR BRANCH, 1998, P. XI

Family, school, and community engagement in the context of serving the academic and social needs of a diverse school population requires *mindful intentional-ness* on the part of educators. Yes, you read that phrase correctly, *mindful intentional-ness*. It is our experience that one must be aware of a need in order to be mindful, and once awareness is piqued it must be followed by action, ergo we create the term, *intentional-ness*. Please understand this is not just cutesy play with current, fashionable words. No, it is our experience that too often family and community members, with particular focus on communities of color and communities of modest to low incomes, are not well served by their local schools. Far too often such communities have been marginalized in ways, intentionally or unintentionally, schools communicate that they are not interested in meaningful family, school, and community engagement.

There are at least two good reasons for educators to be interested in parent and family engagement. Fullan's (2003) moral imperative presented in Chapter 2 has educators serving our diverse communities in ways that address inequities as the right thing to do. Should moral persuasion not be sufficient, maybe legal mandates provide motivation to do what is legal and right. The two most recent iterations of the Elementary and Secondary Education Act (ESEA), No Child Left Behind (NCLB; 2002) and Every Student Succeeds Act (ESSA; 2015), mandate that all schools and school districts have plans to expressly address achievement disparities and to provide resources in support of schools' and school districts' efforts. Similarly, as stated earlier in Chapter 3, many states have enacted laws such as California's 2013 Local Control Funding Formula (LCFF) and Local Control Accountability Plan (LCAP) as state expectations and resources that require attention to and progress with closing access/opportunity and achievement gaps.

Experience tells us that in some schools and school districts, family, school, and community engagement are a tradition that dates back generations. In such schools, families and community members are involved as partners in all aspects of school life. Engagement includes being active in school board elections, participating in parent-teacher organizations, serving as members of school site councils, volunteering for school events such as bake sales and chaperoning school events, and voting in local elections. In schools and districts where events like these are routine, family and community engagement are part of the DNA of the school and the community it serves. The very culture of the school exudes family and community engagement (Henderson, Johnson, Mapp, & Davies, 2007).

In schools where family and community engagement is being introduced for the first time or resurrected after a period of dormancy, processes have to be devised and initiated wherein members of the school community reach out to families and community members. In schools without the tradition of family and community engagement, school people have had to be intentional in reaching out to family and community members. A variation of *reaching out* in schools with diverse populations is expanding family and community engagement to include racial or ethnic groups from the community not historically involved in school activities.

We recognize Joyce Epstein's, Steve Constantino's, and Karen Mapp & Paul Kuttner's roles in providing educators with time-tested methods for family, school, and community engagement. In this chapter, we align the Essential Elements of Cultural Proficiency with their works.

ALIGNMENTS

This chapter describes the alignment of Cultural Proficiency's Essential Elements with Epstein's Six Types of Parent Involvement, Constantino's Five Simple Principles, and Mapp & Kuttner's Dual-Capacity Building Framework. The matrix that is Table 4.1, Alignment of Cultural Proficiency, Epstein, Constantino, and Mapp & Kuttner portrays the alignment of the four frameworks.

CULTURAL PROFICIENCY'S GUIDING PRINCIPLES PROVIDE A MORAL BASE FOR ESSENTIAL ELEMENTS

The Guiding Principles of Cultural Proficiency illustrate the manner in which (1) educators' core values and (2) their schools' policies are intended to inform and guide their actions. The Essential Elements of Cultural Competence/Proficiency inform educators' equitable and inclusive behaviors and actions as well as the schools' practices. The Guiding Principles provide moral and ethical direction in educators' carefully and intentionally developing core values to lead their and their school's actions. The Essential Elements are five action phrases to be used in guiding educators' pursuit of being equitable and inclusive in designing and executing family and community engagement efforts.

USING OUR ASSETS OF MORAL AUTHORITY, REFLECTION, AND DIALOGUE

Reflection and dialogue are educators' asset-based strategies known to focus on how to best serve the needs of students and, yet, are too rarely applied to our roles as educational leaders. The asset-based resource for schools and school districts to rely on is the moral authority and responsibility of doing what is right for our students (Fullan, 2003; Bromberg & Theokas, 2013). When we recognize skillful reflection and dialogue as assets in combination with the moral authority behind well-thought-out approaches to strategic planning and professional development, reflection and dialogue serve as bridges for closing persistent and historical learning gaps extant among the demographic groups of our students.

TABLE 4.1

Alignments of Cultural Proficiency, Epstein, Constantino, and Mapp & Kuttner

Epstein	Constantino	Mapp & Kuttner	Cultural Proficiency Family, School, and Community Engagement
	Culture that engages every family	The challenge (Ineffective Family-School Partnerships)	**Culture/language**
Communicating	Communicate effectively and build relationships	⇩	**Communicating**
		Opportunity Conditions	**Caring/ relationships**
Learning at home		⇩	
Decision making	Engage every family in decision making	Policy and Program Goals	**Collective responsibility**
Collaborating with the community	Engage the greater community	⇩	**Collaboration community**
Parenting		Family and Staff Capacity (Effective Family-School Partnerships-Supporting School Achievement & School Improvement	
Volunteering			**Connectedness**
	Empower every family		

GUIDING PRINCIPLES OF CULTURAL PROFICIENCY: SURFACING OUR ASSUMPTIONS, BELIEFS, AND VALUES

We invite you to read the following nine questions and employ your skills of reflection and dialogue. First, read each question and *reflect* on your personal responses. Ask yourself, what is my truthful, honest response to each question? Your responses are to surface your deeply held assumptions and beliefs that inform your values about the cultural communities you serve. Educational leaders who are willing to look deep within themselves to examine the *why* of *how* they developed certain attitudes, beliefs, and values are well prepared to lead schools serving diverse communities.

Second, in your role as school leader—county, district, or site level—we invite you to engage with your colleagues in *dialogue* to surface deeply held assumptions and reach shared understanding of what narrowing and closing opportunity/access and learning gaps mean to the school community. Inclusive dialogue sessions can lead to statements of shared beliefs and values about all students learning. The nine questions guide educators and school districts to inquire, surface, and understand their core values in working the rich diversity found in their school communities.

Nine Key Questions for Reflection and Dialogue

- To what extent do you honor culture as a natural and normal part of the community you serve?

- To what extent do you recognize and understand the differential and historical treatment accorded to those least well served in our schools?

- When working with people whose culture is different from you, to what extent do you see the person as both an individual and as a member of a cultural group?

- To what extent do you recognize and value the differences within the cultural communities you serve?

- To what extent do you know and respect the unique needs of cultural groups in the community you serve?

- To what extent do you know how cultural groups in your community define family and the manner in which family serves as the primary system of support for students?

- To what extent do you recognize and understand the bicultural reality for cultural groups historically not well served in our schools?

- To what extent do you recognize your role in acknowledging, adjusting to, and accepting cross-cultural interactions as necessary social and communications dynamics?

- To what extent do you incorporate cultural knowledge into educational practices and policy-making? (Lindsey, Terrell, Nuri, & Lindsey, 2010)

Reflection

After responding to the nine questions, what was your initial reaction to reading the questions? What is your reaction—thinking and/or feeling—now that you have completed the task? Please use the space below to record your thinking.

_____

_____

_____

_____

BEING INTENTIONAL IN VALUING STUDENTS' CULTURES AS ASSETS

Opportunity/access and achievement gaps are challenges that must bring educators, parents, families, and community members together in committed partnerships. As stated previously, the gaps are not new; they are historical, they are persistent, and they are on our doorsteps to address and resolve.

An initial step on the part of a school and school district is to move away from responding to learning gaps as compliance issues and to use the transparency afforded by talking about the gaps as a means for transforming school culture through school leaders using their internal assets of reflection and dialogue. Educators' personal reflections on their practice and engagement in purposeful dialogue with colleagues, parents, and members of the community on topics of student success facilitate constructive change.

Thoughtful discussion of the questions can provide the basis for developing mission statements and core values intended to serve a diverse community. Strong core personal and organizational values are the basis of effective school organizations (Collins & Porras, 1997; Senge et al., 2000; Terrell & Lindsey, 2009). Coupled with one's personal core values, the values implicit in Cultural Proficiency's nine guiding principles can serve as the underpinning for developing inclusive and equitable schools and school districts.

VALUING LEADS TO DOING

A word of caution: Convening and developing the vision, mission, and core value statements is a necessary and powerful beginning, but it is only that—a beginning. Core values are intended to guide our actions. Core values give rise to coherent standards for personal and institutional conduct. For the individual educator, vision, mission, and core value statements are intended to influence and guide our behaviors;

for schools and school districts, core values are to guide development of institutional policies and practices. The Essential Elements of Cultural Competence/Proficiency are standards derived from the Guiding Principles and as such inform most every action to be taken by an educator, school, or school district. The Essential Elements are an interrelated set of standards:

- **Assessing Cultural Knowledge**—identifying the cultural groups present in the school and system.

- **Valuing Diversity**—developing an appreciation for the differences within and among cultural groups.

- **Managing the Dynamics of Difference**—learning to respond appropriately and effectively to the issues that arise in a diverse environment.

- **Adapting to Diversity**—changing and adopting new policies and practices that support diversity, equity, and inclusion.

- **Institutionalizing Cultural Knowledge**—drive changes into the systems of the organization.

(Lindsey, Thousand, Jew, & Piowlski, 2018, pp. 28–29)

Knowledge of one's core values as revealed when considering the Guiding Principles and embracing the Essential Elements as standards for our work is further informed by the practical suggestions afforded by three (shown in bold type) of Epstein's Six Types of Parent Involvement in this example.

Beginning With Families

A THEORETICAL FRAMEWORK MODEL FOR FAMILY, SCHOOL, AND COMMUNITY PARTNERSHIPS

Using their weekend Saturday (instead of resting), over eighty parents and their children met for an all-day Saturday School, Family, and Community Engagement workshop planned by students, parents, college professors, local university student affairs staff, and community social service and business agencies. These workshops were organized and led by the middle school college counselor and designed by parents, teachers, students, and school staff. The goal was to empower parents and their children (fourth through eighth and ninth through twelfth) to explore college to career opportunities and pathways. Workshops focused on how parents and their children can attend local community colleges and meet the requirements for admissions to the California State University, the University of California, as well as private and independent colleges. Workshops included admissions, financial aid, transfer of college credit from another country, health clinic, financial and budgeting, and motivational

(Continued)

(Continued)

speakers. All workshops were in Spanish and English. This idea was initiated by the school's college counselor in Spring 2018, at Eje Academy, a dual language immersion school in El Cajon, California. It grew out of the concern that many of their graduating eighth grade students who were entering the various feeder high schools were not getting enrolled in college preparation course requirements or completing financial aid applications in their senior year. Other small charter K–8 schools were experiencing the same obstacles. By Fall 2018, another college counselor at Nativity Preparatory School replicated the same school, family, and community engagement model entitled "Community Success Day" where 101 middle school and high school students, and parents, attended the event.

This story illustrates an example of co-created, collaborative, and diverse family, school, and community decision making. The families and community members voiced their concerns, and the schools listened. Communication was open and the result was the shared development of culturally relevant workshops offered in two languages. This is clearly an example of *collaborating with the community*, *decision making*, and *communication* as elements of successful planning for partnerships.

Joyce Epstein and colleagues have documented the importance of developing partnerships between families, schools, and communities in educational research, policy, and practice (Epstein 1991, 2015; Epstein & Dauber, 1991). Epstein constructed a typology of family involvement with a focus on how involvement by families can be part of different family involvement methods and practices in and out of school.

- **Type 1: Parenting.** Includes basic obligations of families, involves parenting skills, including assisting students' health and safety and supporting and maintaining of home conditions that assist learning and student behavior throughout the students' school attendance.

- **Type 2: Communication.** The role of schools entails clear and consistent communication between the school and families as it relates to school academic programs as well as students' social emotional progress. The use of communication methods includes home visits, telephone calls or other forms of technology-based communication devices, parent-teacher conferences, and written communication by notes, emails, and newsletters.

- **Type 3: Volunteer.** This entails family involvement at the school site itself and includes assisting educators in and out of the classroom, assisting administrators, supporting students in classrooms, and attendance and volunteering at school activities. This type of family involvement is the most traditional form of parent involvement in our schools.

- **Type 4: Learning at Home.** Requires that educators guide and support parents in monitoring, assisting, or participating in learning type activities at home. Educators work with parents on how to review, monitor, and help with homework and construct home activities by involving parents and making sure the homework activities are coordinated with school curriculum.

- **Type 5: Decision Making.** Embraces school governance as advocacy for both students and families. The decision-making type also involves parents and community members engaged in processes that mold the way in which schools operate by providing families with an opportunity to have their voices valued and heard in the decisions across the varied groups in our schools such as Parent Teacher Associations or Parent Teacher Organizations, school boards, and community advocacy groups.

- **Type 6: Collaboration.** Includes working with profit and nonprofit community organizations and businesses. This type focuses on the role of the school in building community partnerships with businesses, cultural and social organizations, and other groups that provide school and community resources to improve students' education and academic and vocational programs.

Epstein's typology reflects and is informed by the historical, legal, and educational bases that inform modern American schooling. In-depth knowledge of the six types of family involvement enables educators to learn and apply the Cultural Proficiency dispositions and skills needed to engage our varied and diverse families in the education of their children and youth.

Our focus on access, equity, and inclusion for Cultural Proficiency, coupled with relationship building for the family, school, and community engagement framework drive the essence of this book. Therefore, from Epstein's six types, we selected Communicating, Decision Making, and Collaborating With Community as being particularly aligned with the Essential Elements of Cultural Competence and Proficiency.

Communicating with families and communities is extremely important considering that in order for any relationship to thrive, effective communication has to take place. Of course, communication can appear in various forms, such as written, verbal, or nonverbal, but nevertheless, communication is crucial when initiating contact with families, valuing diversity, building trust, and resolving conflict. It's part of the initial relationship building process (Dettmer, Knackendoffel, & Thurston, 2012).

Decision making is a process in which deliberation takes place at some level, usually before an action takes place. Within the process of decision making, factors are considered, pros and cons are weighed, and possible outcomes are discussed and reviewed. At the forefront of decision making for this book is the process of having equitable opportunities for different voices to be included in decision-making processes, for every aspect of schools, education, and students' schooling experiences. Decision making impacts providing materials, spending funds, and developing policies, for example. Having a say in what happens and how it happens aligns with fairness and being able to partake in making informed decisions with an equal voice (Shapiro & Stefkovish, 2016).

Collaborating with community is a critical component to student outcomes and achievement. Working together in relationship with each other builds strong connections. Collaborating itself denotes a sense of equity in relationships. No one or nothing is greater or lesser than the other. The education of the child allows for multiple influences to contribute to the success of multiple entities—students, schools, families, and communities. School personnel and families collaboratively work with the neighborhood and business communities combining resources to promote and positively impact the entire educational system, thus relationally collaborating and building community.

Constantino's Five Simple Principles

1 – A culture that engages every family

2 – Communicate effectively and build relationships

3 – Empower every family

4 – Engage every family in decision making

5 – Engage the greater community

Constantino's model impacts the family, school, and community scholarly and practical arenas due to the addition and consideration of culture. He posits that culture impacts every aspect of student learning. He expands the definition of culture to mean the culture of schools, the culture of neighborhoods, and the culture of communities. Cultural Proficiency's Essential Element of Valuing Diversity aligns well with Constantino's model.

Reflection

In what ways do Epstein's and Constantino's work inform your understanding of family and community engagement? Please use the space provided to record your response.

_____

_____

_____

_____

DUAL CAPACITY-BUILDING FRAMEWORK

Throughout the years, educators and families have voiced the desire to work together and share the responsibility of educating children. There are many reasons, though, why the execution of these desires has not been fulfilled. Negative assumptions are created from both sides, and fingers are pointed at each other to blame for students not achieving. In summary, educators give several reasons for this problem.

First, educators realize that their training in becoming an educator did not adequately prepare them for working with families of diverse backgrounds. While education programs focus primarily on preparing prospective teachers to teach, counselors to counsel and advise, and administrators to lead and guide, they are sometimes lacking in preparing educators to work with families.

Second, educators have historically struggled with their own biases of working with families with diverse backgrounds. Many educators have voiced that they simply do not know how to work with diverse families. Research about educator biases indicates that educators often view families with diverse backgrounds from a deficit lens. This deficit lens approach contributes to a lack of respect for families' cultures and values, and a disregard for a family's social and cultural capital (Louque & Latunde, 2014; Thompson, 2003).

Parents and families have also struggled with partnering with schools. Historically, families who are from diverse backgrounds are often faced with unwelcoming district and school staff. Even when families volunteer or attend meetings, they often report how their voices aren't heard and their opinions are not valued (Leadership Conference Education Fund, 2017; Mapp & Kuttner, 2013; Weiss, Bouffard, Bridglall, & Gordon, 2009).

The dual capacity framework (Mapp & Kuttner, 2013) emphasizes that partnerships between families and schools must focus on building the capacities in both educators and families for the purpose of engaging more collectively and effectively with each other. Capacity is described using four components: capabilities, connections, confidence, and cognition. For educators, learning more about the communities and families they serve provides an opportunity to better connect with students. Training and building knowledge about families' and communities' funds of knowledge is paramount to building trust and mutual respect. For families, being included in policy and program development increases their knowledge base and awareness about their children's schools. They also need information on student learning, college access, and the operationalization of the school system.

The Dual Capacity-Building Framework is formulated using the following components:

1. A description of the capacity challenges that must be addressed to support the cultivation of effective home-school partnerships;

2. An articulation of the conditions integral to the success of family-school partnership initiatives and interventions;

3. An identification of the desired intermediate capacity goals that should be the focus of family engagement policies and programs at the federal, state, and local level; and

4. A description of the capacity-building outcomes for school and program staff as well as for families (Mapp & Kuttner, 2013, p. 7).

Incorporating and connecting to these capacity-building systems is a part of what culturally proficient educators do. Culturally proficient educators' approach to capacity building expands the responsibility and accountability of student learning to family, school, and community engagement. Valuing families' diverse backgrounds, respecting their cultural capital, and acknowledging their funds of knowledge when initiating policies and programs increases positive structural, systemic, and sustainable change.

For families, institutionalizing knowledge so they can truly be a part of the process is crucial to building their confidence in school personnel. Educating families on how students learn, sharing school processes, and explaining policies and procedures ensures them being better acquainted with the school culture (Mapp, 2018).

To diminish some of the miscommunication, misidentification, and misguided practices in schools, educators are encouraged to not only work on themselves with Cultural Proficiency but also to reach out in other ways for assistance. Creating dual capacity opportunities within the schools using professional development with their staff, as well as creating opportunities outside the schools with families, churches, and the community, builds trust and engaging opportunities for every constituent of the school environment (Clark-Louque & Latunde, 2019; Mapp, 2018).

Research on promising practices for home-school partnerships that improve student outcomes and sustain positive relationships suggests a dual capacity-building framework. School leaders can apply a dual capacity-building framework to provide teachers and parents with goals and principles to follow as they execute partnerships. The goals of the framework are to increase the capabilities, connections, cognition, and confidence of all parties involved (Mapp, 2018; Mapp & Kuttner, 2013; Weiss, Lopez, & Rosenberg, 2010).

The 7 Cs of Culturally Proficient Family, School, and Community Engagement

From the alignments of Cultural Proficiency, Epstein, Constantino, and Mapp & Kuttner, we derived the 7 Cs Framework of Family, School, and Community Engagement:

- Collaboration
- Communication
- Caring/Compassion
- Culture
- Community
- Connectedness
- Collective Responsibility

Dialogic Questions

With your grade level team, departmental team, or schoolwide team members, look around the group and discuss who has not been invited to this conversation. Once you have identified the roles of those not invited to the conversation, take a few moments to discuss next steps for involving others in the conversation. Once you have identified those persons or their roles, what might be next steps for your group? Use the space provided to record your responses and to being an outline of next steps.

_____

_____

_____

_____

SUMMARY

This chapter presented the four conceptual approaches: Cultural Proficiency, Epstein's six types of involvement, Constantino's five principles of engagement, and Mapp and Kuttner's dual capacity-building framework. Three of the six types of involvement, one of the five principles, and two of the four main dual-capacity components are the common focus areas. These focus areas demonstrate and support the main premises of Cultural Proficiency, which are access, equity, and inclusion.

LOOKING AHEAD: CHAPTER 5

Chapter 5 leads you into the next phase of creating and building effective family, school, and community engagements and partnerships. A conceptually based framework, *The Seven Cs of Culturally Proficient Family, School, and Community Engagement*, will be introduced. The seven Cs are (1) Collaboration, (2) Communication, (3) Caring/ Compassion, (4) Culture, (5) Community, (6) Connectedness, and (7) Collective Responsibility. This framework will provide you with an approach for examining your own values, beliefs, and behaviors of policies as well as practices that are part of your school or district. These tools will guide your continued professional learning as an educator on how to best plan, implement, and evaluate family, school, and community engagement and partnerships so you may serve and engage all families.

The 7 Cs of Engagement

*The greatness of a community is most accurately measured by the
compassionate actions of its members.*

—CORETTA SCOTT KING (JANUARY 17, 2000), LA TIMES, AP

Now that you've learned (or reviewed) the Tools of Cultural Proficiency and
know the basis for our moral imperative to educate all students to high
levels, you have taken yet another step toward individual, organizational, and
systemic change. By establishing and expanding your knowledge and facil-
ity in use of the Tools, you are ready to go forth and work with colleagues to
develop an accessible, equitable, and inclusive family, school, and community
engagement school environment. The 7 Cs are intended to function as support concepts for framing and cultivating strong family-school-community
partnerships. Assessing your baseline data of where you and your school are
on the Cultural Proficiency Continuum (Chapter 1) will lead you in how
to proceed in revising, changing, and eliminating (some) practices and policies in favor of actions that lead to an increasingly culturally competent and
proficient school.

Epstein's model is valued for the six types of involvement, Constantino's sets
forth the five principles of engagement, and Mapp & Kuttner's Dual Capacity-
Building Framework envelops school and community members. To Epstein's,
Constantino's, and Mapp & Kuttner's models, we integrate seven skills and con-
cepts for effective family and community engagement. They are a reflection of
leadership literature that encourages equity, inclusion, and building relationships
(Lindsey, Nuri-Robins, Terrell, & Lindsey, 2018) in concert with significant indi-
cators of positive family, school, and community relationships (Boonk, Gijselaers,
Ritzen, & Brand-Gruwel, 2018; Constantino, 2003; Epstein, 2011; Mapp &
Kuttner, 2013).

We present these knowledge-based concepts and skills in Table 5.1 Tools for
Cultural Proficiency and 7 Cs for Engagement and briefly discuss why researchers
and practitioners feel that they're important. We also include the impact or possible
downfalls if they are not considered or included. The seven concepts are collaboration, communication, caring/compassion, culture, community, connectedness, and
collective responsibility (Table 5.1).

TABLE 5.1

Tools for Cultural Proficiency and 7 Cs for Engagement

Tools for Cultural Proficiency	7 Cs Concepts for Engagement
Essential Elements	Collaboration
Guiding Principles	Communication
Proficiency Continuum	Caring/Compassion
Overcoming Barriers	Culture
	Community
	Connectedness
	Collective Responsibility

COLLABORATION

Collaboration is "when members of an inclusive learning community work together as equals to assist students to succeed in the classroom" (US Department of State, 2019, https://www.state.gov/m/a/os/43980.htm). This definition is grounded in Friend and Cook's (1992, pp. 6–28) list of key components for successful collaboration:

1. Collaboration is voluntary.
2. Collaboration requires parity among participants.
3. Collaboration is based on mutual goals.
4. Collaboration depends on shared responsibility for participation.
5. Individuals who collaborate share their resources.
6. Individuals who collaborate share accountability for outcomes.

Collaboration as a norm in the school and district contributes to the smooth operation of the school for effective team building and improved student outcomes. Developing collaborative skills is important for school leaders interacting daily with colleagues, family members, and students. Most importantly, individuals collaborate voluntarily to share common interests and goals. Collaborative participants contribute their suggestions, and their input is valued and recognized as a crucial element of the engagement process. Mutual goals are the focus while each member contributes their own share of ideas, resources, and accountability of outcomes. With *collaboration*, every stakeholder's contribution is welcomed and is an integral component of productive engagement and is of utmost importance when bringing together diverse cultural constituencies.

In collaborative culturally inclusive relationships, family and community members must feel safe to participate deeply in regular meetings, decision-making processes, and school reform. True collaboration and inclusion are evident through respectful dialogue and interaction while building feelings of belonging. A culture of *collaboration* modelled by culturally proficient school leaders fosters trust and respect, as well as continuous improvement of family and community engagement practices. *Collaboration* leads to positive rapport, effective communication, and mutual respect and is an important skill in creating positive relationships and events (US Department of State, 2019).

Failure to *collaborate* is easy to detect and has social and legal ramifications. Failure to collaborate runs the risk of hurt feelings, combativeness, and resistance and can erode trust among families, community members, and schools when members are not included in meetings, policy development, and decisions (Olender, Elias, & Mastroleo, 2010).

Failure to *collaborate* effectively negatively impacts the efforts to build relationships and often leads to districts being out of compliance with federal education mandates and guidelines. The Individuals with Disabilities Act (IDEA), and the Every Student Succeeds Act (ESSA) as described in Chapter 2, require home-school *collaboration*. These mandates are based in home-school collaboration being linked to positive student academic achievement outcomes.

Reflection

Take a few moments and think about the collaborative activities your school and district engage in with the culturally diverse families and communities served by your school or district. In what ways do you describe the engagement with the various communities? Please use the space below to record your thinking.

COMMUNICATION

Communication is derived from the Latin word *communicare*, which means *to share*. Communication is "the giving and receiving or sharing of anything . . . a cooperative enterprise requiring the mutual interchange of ideas and information, and out of which understanding develops and action taken" (Moore, Bagin, & Gallagher, 2012, p. 70). *Communication* is a continuous process critical to establishing collaborative activities (Green, 2008). In establishing partnerships with culturally diverse families and communities, clear communication is evident when expectations are expressed and serve to guide effective partnerships. Clear expectations surface through thoughtful discussions that help heighten trust and lower distrust. Consistent, clear, and continuous communication help realign courses of action to focus on equitable partnerships focused on meeting student-centered goals.

School leaders must be able to communicate in ways that families and community members are open to being receptive. As we've all experienced at one time or another, it's not always what we say, but how we say it. No matter the subject or topic of our statements, our tone, volume, and manner of word usage can greatly influence how a message is perceived and received.

Effective *communication* involves the use of effective and appropriate strategies that result in expanded collaboration experiences. It is no surprise that collaboration and *communication* are intricately intertwined. Collaborative communication strategies such as speaking in noninflammatory language and practicing bidirectional *communication* fosters and promotes collaboration skills. Effective *communication* strategies that foster collaboration include listening, providing a safe environment, engaging in ongoing and consistent communications, and using a variety of communication methods (Dettmer, Thurston, Knackendoffel, & Dyck, 2009; Weller & Weller, 2002). Basic communication parameters such as these serve as reminders in taking responsibility for communicating with our diverse communities:

- The main element of effective *communication* remains to be *listening.* In order to authentically hear what families are saying, we must listen empathically and *hear* the depth of their words and messages.

- A *safe environment* is imperative for people to share "assumptions, prior experiences, and fears. Creating an environment for collaboration by developing, agreeing to, and posting meeting ground rules that will facilitate open communication" helps to develop a framework for building trust for future interactions and collaborative opportunities (Green, 2008, p. 14).

- *Ongoing and consistent communication* indicates interest and connectedness. Spending time reaching out to families and community members consistently reinforces intentionality and purpose. Inviting family members to participate at different levels of school events helps families make choices in types of participation and areas of interest.

- *Variety of methods of communication* to meet families' communication styles. Sending letters home with students was once a reliable method of disseminating information to families. That's not necessarily the case today. Today social media expands the range of opportunities for reaching the ever-larger audiences and increases the possibilities of responses when important (Dettmer, Knackendoffel, & Thurston, 2012).

The benefits of effective *communication* are numerous. Effective *communication* opens opportunities for shared dialogue and results in an exchange of ideas, responses, and interactions. Bidirectional communication encourages responses from families with different backgrounds, languages, and culture. Empathic listening communicates caring and adds value to the message. As a result, families can be more confident and willing to express their concerns. Effective communication builds rapport and relationships with families and community members.

For schools in the twenty-first century, various forms of *communication* are needed to reach families from diverse cultures and socioeconomic backgrounds. Failure to recognize the need for print or oral communication in different languages and different formats could mean a missed conference time or a missed opportunity for children to have family members present at a performance. The risk of ineffective forms of communication can result in community members feeling isolated and excluded, thereby creating an unfortunate impediment in reaching engagement goals intended to support student academic and social success.

To succinctly provide guidance for achieving effective *communication,* Table 5.2, The Flamboyan Foundation's *Communicating With Families About Academics–Do's and Don'ts* chart (2011) is presented as a tool with illustrated responses to use when communicating with families. The Do's column represents best strategies for use in communicating with families and community members. Examples demonstrate respectful ways to ensure clear, plain language is used, positive comments are made, and practical and actionable steps are taken when sharing information with families. Responses in the Don'ts column are provided as a means for contrasting those responses that are too often uttered, wittingly or not, by some school members. Awareness is an initial component of being intentional in building effective cross-cultural communication behaviors and strategies.

TABLE 5.2

Communicating With Families About Academics—Do's and Don'ts

	Do	Don't
Manageable for teachers and families	• Pick something that you are already assessing or doing. • Pick information that you think is most important for your families to know. • Keep your analysis and learning support recommendations short and sweet.	• Collect new information simply to send it home. • Share information on every single academic subject and standard. • Send a long, written explanation of the child's data and five suggested activities per week for parents to support learning.
Regular	• Share information on a consistent basis; it doesn't have to be every week. • Pick how often you will be sharing information and stick to it so parents know when to expect it.	• Share information only at parent-teacher conferences or through report cards. • Over-commit and spend more time than you have sending home information to families.

	Do	Don't
Explicitly explained to families	• Use an event where you have many families in your classroom, such as back-to-school night, to share your data-sharing system with families. • Follow up with families who did not attend your training on your system to make sure they understand it. • Ensure your students understand what's going home to their families so they can explain it to them as well.	• Assume families will understand the data or information you are sending home without an explanation. • Forget about families who aren't responsive to or interested in the system at first. • Start sending information to families without explaining it to students.
Positive	• Start any communication about academics with a student strength. • Cast students' struggling within an optimistic light—"challenges, areas for growth, etc."	• Only list things the student needs help with. • Make student performance sound dismal and impossible to improve.
Transparent and placed in context	• Provide perspective—what is the class average? The state average? • How does the information relate to progress toward a student's goal?	• Share information in a vacuum. (For example, Daiquann is a Level "F" in reading. Parents won't usually know what an F means for their student's grade level.)
Clear, plain language	• Tell parents what standards or skills mean in everyday language. • Provide visual examples—copies of books, math problems, scenarios, etc., that illustrate what scores or levels mean. (For example, Daiquann reads "F" level books. This is what an "F" level book looks like. It has 3–5 sentences and a picture that clearly illustrates the sentences. Many of the words have the same sounds or letter patterns.)	• Write standards verbatim. • Share only numbers or levels with families without visual aids or explanations.
Actionable	• Give parents one or two concrete suggestions on how they can accelerate learning at home. • Tailor each suggestion to a specific skill a student needs to work on to improve the score. (For example, understand the difference between addition and subtraction, read fluently without stopping to break up words, etc.)	• Provide no action steps for parents to take to help their kid's data improve. • Give generic suggestions like "read with your child."

(Continued)

(Continued)

	Do	Don't
Check for and sustain family understanding	• Ask parents to write comments or questions on the information and send them back to you so you can confirm they've read it. • Follow up by phone or in person with families who are not providing written confirmation they receive and/ or understand the material. • If using an online grade book, track how often parents log on and reach out to those who don't by phone, email, or personal contact.	• Ask parents for a signature only. • Send information home and have no way to follow up or check who received it.

Source: Flamboyan Foundation—Communicating with Families—flamboyanfoundation.org

CARING

Louis, Murphy, & Smylie (2016) define caring leadership as ". . . a broader concept that must take into consideration caring for students (direct interactions that manifest a caring culture), caring for community (recognizing and respecting parent and community values and resources), and caring for a broader variety of student outcomes (p. 337). *Caring* is built over time and is an outgrowth of numerous person-to-person experiences. Noddings (2005) noted that increased caring behavior helps one to relate better to others. Noddings's (1992) work on an ethic of care describes a reciprocal relationship of "one caring" and the "one cared for." Noddings notes that in educational settings, promoting the "I must do something" attitude takes precedent over the "something must be done" approach. This means that student care is the responsibility of not only the parents and families, but the teachers, counselors, administrators, and all school personnel. In examples of *care*, we have witnessed educators staying after school motivating students, nurturing students, and actively demonstrating their genuine concern for students. Students want educators to care and to "be present" (Clark-Louque, Greer, Clay, & Balogun, 2017; Thompson, 2002).

Ethical *caring* and compassion supports positive, long-lasting partnerships. When educators show compassion to families and community members, it leads to those members believing the school is a supportive environment. When working with families and communities, a compassionate mindset takes courage of conviction. Being calm and listening to families lets families know that their voices are heard, their side of the story is valued, and consequences assigned due to instances of student misbehaviors are fair and equitable. Culturally proficient educators strive for caring communities and for socially just communities (Nieto & Bode, 2012).

In school environments lacking in compassion, decisions are made with little or no thought of how it will impact others. It only takes one uncaring comment or response to cause irreparable damage to someone's self-esteem and attitude (Strarrat, 1994).

In a study of 228 undergraduate students on respectful and disrespectful instructor behavior, Buttner's (2004) findings indicate that when students are not treated with care or respect, they are more apt to behave negatively. In the study, students responded by "not showing up for class, not participating in class discussions, showing less interest in the course topic, and they also made it clear that their self-esteem was negatively impacted" (p. 18).

Reflection

What might be examples of building a systemic infrastructure for demonstrating care and compassion in your school or district? What might be some of the barriers to building such an infrastructure? In what ways do you experience support for caring and compassion?

Please use the space below to record your responses.

_____

_____

_____

_____

CULTURE

The definition of *culture* we use has culture as a set of core values, established practices, and norms. We use the term *culture* when referring to the organizational culture of school as well as to the varied racial, ethnic, social, religious, and related groups represented by the families and communities served by your school or district. Understanding your school's culture is important for developing into a school culture you aspire to have or be (Lindsey, Nuri-Robins, Terrell, & Lindsey, 2018).

In creating a *culture* for strong family and community engagement, positive interactions within the school and with the diverse families and communities being served by the schools are a must. Each and every interaction by school personnel with community members is an opportunity to demonstrate ways in which school culture reflects values for families and communities.

School *culture* can be evident on campus, throughout neighborhoods, and in business and civic organizations. It is displayed in mission statements, slogans, and language. It's a part of the way things are done on a school campus or in a community environment (Gruenert & Whitaker, 2015). The diverse and varied cultures served by our schools provides opportunity for the school culture to embrace the varied groups that make up the school community.

When school *cultures* are not inclusive, or not evident in the day-to-day conduct of schooling, those who are marginalized do not know what are acceptable or unacceptable behaviors. The question that will inevitably arise is, "What did I do wrong?" or "I thought this was acceptable." The absence of an inclusive *culture* may indicate a toxic culture is brewing, and "encourages individuals to see failures as the inevitable results of circumstances outside of their control rather than as opportunities for improvement" (Gruenert & Whitaker, 2015, p. 21). When positive culture is not present, disconcerting and discouraging comments can become the reins that guide and drive the school.

Reflection

To what extent does your school honor cultures in the communities your school serves as a natural and normal part of your school? In what ways do you recognize and value the differences within and among the cultural communities you serve? In what ways does your school incorporate cultural knowledge into its policies, practices, and procedures?

COMMUNITY

Every *community* has its own identity. Demographic information is an important foundational aspect of a community. As discussed earlier in Chapters 1 and 2, educators must know and understand the *community* they serve. Knowing about the culture, demographics, and community organizations provides insight into what the community values as well as how the community functions. *Community* values are represented in the daily activities conducted in the community, what stores and businesses are thriving in the community, and how problems are resolved. Having knowledge about the community helps with the planning of school activities. The more educators know all demographic aspects of their community, the better prepared they will be in serving the educational needs of the *community*. Being visible in the *community* speaks to the extent to which culturally proficient leaders value the community and what the community contributes to the school's identity and successes (Harvard Family Research Project, 2003; Reform Support Network, 2014).

Effective, sustained engagement with the *community* opens many doors to students' and families' education, work, and life opportunities. Employment opportunities are narrowed if *community* ties are missing or severed. Neighborhood schools lead to hiring opportunities in local businesses and as a primary source of part-time jobs for teenagers to earn spending money and in many cases help financially with their families.

Reflection

Describe the diversity of the community served by your school or district. In what ways might you describe the values of your community? What are some of the changes or trends that you witness in your community? In what ways does your school connect with community resources and services? Please use the space below to record your responses.

_____

_____

_____

_____

CONNECTEDNESS

Connectedness "is an overarching construct that encompasses students' sense of belongingness, integration, and satisfaction with their relationship to their institution . . ." (Jorgensen, Farrell, Fudge, & Pritchard, 2018, p. 76). Further examination of the definition of *connectedness* by the Centers for Disease Control and Prevention (CDC; 2009) posits that *connectedness* is "the belief held by students that adults and peers in the school care about their learning as well as about them as individuals" (p. 1). More extensively, school connectedness is when students feel accepted, valued, and supported by others in the school environment (Kading, 2015). In essence, any person who supportively and caringly interacts with the school environment is connected to it.

The Centers for Disease Control and Prevention (2009) lists four factors that greatly impact *connectedness* for students:

1. Adult support—school personnel are impactful adults in students' social, academic, and psychological well-being;

2. Belonging to a positive peer group;

3. Commitment to education; and a

4. Positive school environment.

Connectedness is important because intentional connections between educators and families create bridges in building trust between and among all parties involved. According to the American Psychological Association (APA; 2018), students who feel connected to their schools report higher levels of emotional well-being, have better academic achievement, are less likely to use drugs, and have better school attendance. Therefore, educators are encouraged to create opportunities to involve families as a means to improve school climate that increases students' sense of connectedness to school. *Connectedness* helps students to learn and stay healthy. Improving school connectedness means including families and community members in all aspects of the educational process.

In sharp contrast, disconnectedness gives rise to increased feelings of alienation or isolation from others, and possibly feelings of not belonging. There's a greater risk of disconnectedness occurring for students with disabilities, students who are gay, lesbian, transgender, or bisexual, and students who are homeless. Culturally proficient leaders look for ways to help students become more connected with caring school adults, peers, and school activities (APA, 2018).

COLLECTIVE RESPONSIBILITY

Collective Responsibility assures that staff, teachers, administrators, families, and school board and community members build a culture of institutionalizing working and learning together for the ultimate goal of student achievement gains for all students (Hirsch, 2010). Learning Forward, formerly known as the National Staff Development Council, advocates that "the most important phrase in Learning Forward's definition of professional learning is '*collective responsibility*'" (p. 1).

Collective responsibility "builds organizational capacity to improve the effectiveness of teaching and learning, grows a sense of collective efficacy and encourages a greater sense of ownership for the quality of students' learning" (Whalan, 2012, p. 2). Lee and Smith (1996) found teachers' collective responsibility was empirically linked to student achievement gains. This study represented almost 10,000 teachers and more than 12,000 students across the United States. Their results indicated that teachers and schools who viewed student learning as a *collective responsibility* created equitable learning across the student body, no matter the academic subject.

Schooling is a demanding profession, which requires the support of those involved. "Responsible teachers send messages to families, write lesson plans, instruct students, assess them, return telephone calls, meet with families, and participate in professional training and development" (Mazzone & Miglionico, 2014, p. 15). Responsible school leaders co-create and implement policies and procedures, lead IEP and student team meetings, and make fiscally sound decisions. Responsible parents, guardians, and family members provide shelter for children, prepare meals for them, clothe them, and assist with educating them. Responsible community members manage upkeep of their properties or living spaces and pay their property taxes. Collective effort is required of constituents from every aspect of the school and community to collectively and integrally participate in students' learning and achievement.

The risk when *collective responsibility* is missing is for individual initiatives to replace collaborative work and resentments to creeping into the environment leading to a lack of accountability and creating a negative culture. When the primary influencers and communities' sources of support are engaged in a student's learning, it broadens the possibilities and advantages for access, equity, and inclusion. Collectively, the bond is strengthened due to intentional outreach to the varied sectors of families, schools, and communities (Hirsch, 2010).

Going Deeper Reflection

How do your school leaders promote collective responsibility for family engagement in your school? How do your school leaders promote collective responsibility for student achievement in your school?

_____

_____

_____

_____

Going Deeper Dialogic Questions

In what ways are the 7 Cs evident in your work as an educator? From reading this chapter, in what ways do you want to continue to grow professionally? What might be some next steps for you to take? Please use the space below to record your responses.

_____

_____

_____

_____

COURAGEOUS ENGAGEMENT

Family and community engagement can be a daunting task for the uninitiated; however, building a culture of community engagement benefits the school and the community. Engagement, by definition, is not a loner sport. For engagement to be successful, engagement necessitates leaders who are willing to work with others to carry out their responsibilities. In doing so, the leader leads through example and by working with others to set high standards for self and others.

The 7 Cs concepts are presented as a means to encourage, educate, and empower us as educators and to guide our ongoing assessment in the attainment of the school or district's goals and objectives. The 7 Cs are intended as means for assessing our efforts, not in evaluating our efforts. They are to be like another "C" word—courage. In the event you or your school are in the initial stages of community engagement or in broadening current efforts in ways that reach out to new demographic groups, please know that feelings of excitement, discomfort, or trepidation are natural and normal.

Culturally proficient educators understand that they must be able to honestly reflect on feelings and dwell with any feelings of discomfort when changing the culture of a school or district. As we begin to shift the culture, we surface our and others' assumptions about the actions we are about to take, particularly if those are in contrast for the way things have been done in the past. Acknowledging and surfacing assumptions about the cultures in your community and the changes under way enable the school community to grow and mature. You, your colleagues, and the community you serve will grow from those experiences.

SUMMARY

As mentioned in Chapter 3, it is our moral responsibility, as authors, to educate and support our school leaders, students, families, and communities. The concepts and skills that compose the 7 Cs are to assist you in your mission to build better and stronger culturally proficient relationships with families and communities.

LOOKING AHEAD: CHAPTER 6

Chapters 6 and 7 portray vignettes that represent the Tools of Cultural Proficiency. The stories in Chapter 6 are presented as stories representing challenging experiences of schools and school leaders that demonstrate the Overcoming Barriers side of the Cultural Proficiency Continuum. The vignettes in Chapter 7 correspond to those in Chapter 6 and represent constructive community engagement experiences.

PART III

From Marginalization to Inclusion

6 Barriers to Family, School, and Community Engagement

There are uses to adversity, and they don't reveal themselves until tested. Whether it's serious illness, financial hardship, or the simple constraint of parents who speak limited English; difficulty can tap unsuspected strength.

—SONIA SOTOMAYOR, 2013, P. 13

This chapter focuses on authors' descriptions of barriers to family and community engagement in vignette form. The vignettes are presented to describe the negative impact of barriers and often inappropriate behavior exhibited by schools and districts when family and community members initiate and maintain engagement and involvement. Two of the four vignettes are authors' personal experiences with the dual roles of being parents and educators. One of the vignettes is an author's experiences and observations working with a high school district. The other vignette is a fictionalized composite of the experiences too many schools are having with *active shooter scares*.

BARRIERS TO CULTURAL PROFICIENCY

As discussed in Chapter 1, Cross et al. (1989) identified barriers to Cultural Proficiency that involve

- Recognizing systemic oppression,
- Recognizing one's sense of privilege and entitlement,
- Overcoming resistance to change, and
- Developing an awareness of the need to adapt to diversity.

One of the great myths of the late twentieth century carried into the twenty-first century is that of public schools failing. The myth of failing schools carries with it indictments of educators, particularly teachers, implicit in reports such as "A Nation at Risk," much like the implicit indictment of students and their cultures in the Coleman Report. Myths are usually shrouded in coded language that buries negative attributions into well-meaning terms like *achievement gaps, disproportionality,* and *inequitable access.* Let us be clear, these are terms to be used but applied in a manner that focuses on school policies and practices and the values and behaviors of us, the educators. Key to developing inclusive schools is the willingness and ability of educators to ensure our values and behaviors and our school policies and practices uncover embedded assumptions that marginalize and exclude students and their families by devaluing their cultures. A first step in such a process includes a willingness to recognize resistance to change within ourselves and our colleagues.

In reality, our schools across the United States are doing as well this year as they were in the heyday years of the 1950s with the students for whom our schools were designed, namely middle-class White students and those who could reasonably aspire to emulate them. As the latter twentieth century unfolded, two dynamics befell communities and schools across the United States—changing demographics and school desegregation (Hawley, 1983; Orfield & Frankenberg, 2007). In too many cases, such as Boston (1974), Detroit (1974), Los Angeles (1981), Atlanta (1961), Birmingham (1963), and New Orleans (1960), middle-class White families fled desegregation whether the desegregation plan was the consequence of a court order or a school district voluntary plan. Across the country, alternative programs were created to accommodate fleeing families and ranged from segregation academies to church schools to suburban flight to the precursors of charter schools.

In too many cases, the schools left behind, whether in rural towns or urban centers across the country, are populated with students from predominately low- and middle-income families of color. Frequently, such students are stigmatized with labels such as being culturally disadvantaged, low socioeconomic status (SES), and special needs populations. It is still not uncommon to hear educators utter phrases like *we could do better if we had different students* and *what can one expect when students come from conditions such as these.*

Yes, these are harsh observations, but they are observations that, when viewed with a culturally proficient lens, fall on us—not on the students and communities our schools are to serve. There is no credible research to indicate students are burdened by their cultures or socioeconomic status in such a way as to be incapable of learning. In fact, there is research to indicate that with the right frame of mind, educators can be successful with all cultural and socioeconomic groups of students (Chenoweth, 2017; Wiggington, 1972).

BARRIERS TO FAMILY, SCHOOL, AND COMMUNITY ENGAGEMENT

Family and community engagement with schools is vital to student learning, yet there are many reasons why family, school, and community engagement is a challenge to initiate and maintain. Barriers to family, school, and community engagement are not difficult to identify. One hindrance often expressed by educators is having the time and opportunity to create an atmosphere and school culture that not only welcomes families but also sees families as an integral part of the school system. Dettmer et al., (2012) posits that *some educators view parents as respondents rather than equal partners.* This causes a sense of *we* and *they;* or *right way* and *wrong way; caring* and *noncaring; I know what's best and right,* and *they don't know or care about what's right.* This limiting attitude promotes a system of hierarchical thinking.

Changes to the family structures are also thought to cause a shift in family and parent engagement. A common perception in society is that family is being defined as a mother, father, and two or more children. As *common* as the perception might be, it is just wrong. Single parent homes, multigenerational families, foster homes, and children with no homes are as common in history as is any other configuration. The composition of families is varied and schools have the opportunity to work with diverse communities. Given the fact that the majority of teachers are middle class and mostly White, the parents they work with in many communities are different from educators' socioeconomic backgrounds and cultures.

An unwelcoming school culture is another stated barrier, as mentioned in Chapter 2. Parents often say they feel unwelcome when attempting to participate in their children's school activities. Work schedules often conflict with school activities. Working parents have many choices to make, and while they may have the desire to participate, they know that they have to pay for their rent or mortgages, and other living expenses. Lack of transportation and child care are other barriers known to cause a strain on strong parent, family, and community engagement with schools.

Reflection

As you think about the barriers discussed here, which resonated for you and your school's community? What barriers do you see in your school or district that are not discussed here?

In what ways might these barriers limit family and community engagement at your school? Please use the space below to record your responses.

_____

_____

_____

_____

Cultural Proficiency is grounded in acknowledging systemic barriers in ways that allow educators and their schools to embrace the Guiding Principles of Cultural Proficiency. These Guiding Principles are viewed as an ethical and moral guide to developing professional and institutional core values. The core values are thus focused on the students and community we have, not the community we used to have or we wish we might have.

Using the Family, School, and Community Engagement Rubric (Chapter 1) as a guide, let's examine authors' vignettes that describe barriers to family and community engagement with schools. Read each vignette and make a determination of how you might describe barriers that family and community members face. In the next chapter, you will have an opportunity to read the authors' experiences of positive, constructive engagement.

A Day "Visiting" School

With close to 2000 students, Crestview Hill High's student population was approximately 74 percent (1,475) Hispanic/Latinx and 12 percent (230) African American. Over 75 percent of the students were on free and reduced-price meals and 16 percent were classified as English learners. The teaching staff was diverse, but the principal and three assistant principals were all White. Crestview Hill High School had only been open for four years when my daughter, Angelique, began her ninth grade year there.

At back-to-school night, I met three other African American parents. We briefly spoke about getting involved as parents of first and second year high schoolers. All three said they wouldn't try to be involved anymore as they had volunteered for various functions already, but were always told that their assistance wasn't needed or that the school activity already had enough parents signed up for the event. I told them that I was planning on attending my daughter Angelique's class soon so that she and I could discuss how to better organize her biology notes.

Later that month, I made an appointment with the biology teacher to come by and observe the class and meet with him afterward during his prep period. On the day of the appointment, I checked into the office using the procedures of signing in and having my picture taken by a web camera, and peeling back the badge to stick to my jacket. I was cleared by the office staff, and since I was familiar with the campus, I walked directly to the classroom. I knocked on the door of the classroom (since all classroom doors are locked during class time), and waited for someone to open the door. A student came to the door, and as I began walking in, the teacher acknowledged me with a quick wave "hello" and motioned for me to enter the room. As I entered the classroom, the teacher showed me where I was to sit. Before I could get comfortable in my seat, two school security officers came to the door. A student let them in the classroom and they both walked toward the teacher, and then pointed at me. Both security guards came toward me and informed me that the principal wanted to see me. "Oh ok," I responded, "I'll stop by to see him when I leave." Thinking nothing of it, I remained seated. They then told me that I couldn't stay in the classroom and that they would escort me back to the front office. "Is there something wrong?" I asked. "Have I done anything wrong?" They responded that all they knew was that I needed to be removed from the class.

Besides feeling embarrassed as I was being escorted out with a security guard on each side of me, I felt enraged. I had been in communication with the teacher to come into the classroom, had followed the check-in procedures of the school, and yet had been made to feel like a criminal. What was my daughter thinking had happened, I wondered? I was also concerned it may have appeared to the students in the classroom that I may have done something wrong and had to be taken to the office to be reprimanded, or that I was a threat, and hence needed to be removed for their safety.

After arriving at the principal's office, he simply asked how was I doing and expressed that he wanted to know what I was doing on campus. I told him the reason why I was on campus and that I was visiting my daughter's class. He then told me that I needed to follow school procedures and contact the teacher ahead of time in order to "visit" on campus.

Examples of an African American parent being removed from a classroom for no apparent reason breeds mistrust and anger between African American parents and school leaders. In analyzing and reflecting on this situation, let's begin with me, the parent in this case. I parked in the appropriate parking area, checked into the office following protocol, received my badge, walked directly to the class and sat in a seat in the classroom (at the direction of the teacher). Even before the actual day at school, I followed procedure by contacting the teacher and asking for permission to attend class. What was so wrong or inappropriate about that?

I began to wonder, "How many other parents made appointments with teachers, only to be removed from the classroom once they got there?" "Were there any other parents who had been escorted to the office by school security officers?" and "How many other parents were African American and had similar experiences?" Now, analyzing the principal's behavior, it is clear that the principal did not want me in the classroom. When I arrived at his office, there was no emergency, and when I asked what was wrong and why I was brought to the office, he said I hadn't done anything wrong. He had just heard that I was on campus.

USING THE FAMILY, SCHOOL, AND
COMMUNITY ENGAGEMENT RUBRIC

Using the rubric as a guide, this principal's actions are located at the Cultural Incapacity point of the continuum. Cultural Incapacity "virtually guarantees limited opportunities and can lead to learned helplessness, which is people's belief that they are powerless to help themselves because of their repeated experiences of disempowerment" (Lindsey, Nuri-Robins, Terrell, & Lindsey, 2018, p. 135). His use of authority as a principal to stop a parent, who had followed established protocol in making an appointment with the biology teacher and in checking in at the office, from checking on the progress of her child is still difficult to comprehend. Why would a principal send security personnel after a parent? You may say fear. Fear of what the parent may find out on campus? Fear of how the parent would interpret whatever she saw? The principal didn't want the parent in the classroom, nor did he want the parent on campus. A few days after this incident, two Latina teachers informed the parent that the principal had stated at a cabinet meeting that they should be careful when this parent comes on campus and no one was allowed to have outside conversations with the parent.

Santa Maria, California—*Leading From the Strawberry Fields—The Backstory*

The fractured relationship that existed between large segments of the Latinx community and the school district was, and is, not unique to the Santa Maria community. I have little doubt this story will resonate with educators in school districts and communities across the United States.

Parents from the Santa Maria High School were very unhappy with what they perceived as low-quality education being accorded to their children. Their parent-community meetings, cafecitos, were community based and often attracted 200+ participants, attendance in direct contrast to the very low turnout for school sponsored PTA meetings. From the cafecito meetings emerged documented grievances that they took to school board meetings where speakers roundly criticized members of the school board, the superintendent, high school administrators, teachers, and the teacher union. It was not unusual to hear allegations of unfair scheduling that favored teachers' preferences over what parents deemed to be in the best interest of their children. Allegations of bias, prejudice, and racism were not uncommon.

In late summer 2010, the district brought in a new high school principal (also a 1993 graduate of Santa Maria High School) and with him, a new assistant principal. These two men had been introduced to Cultural Proficiency by a mentor. In their first year at the high school, their priority was to bring some semblance of order to student attendance and to developing professional learning communities. In that first year, they also recognized the power of the cafecitos and chose to work with the parents and to bring their concerns to the table. Sounds easy enough, doesn't it? Yes, in the abstract any plan they would develop could have been straightforward and easy to implement. However, the relationship between the coterie of parents who led the cafecitos, school district leaders, and members of the teachers and their leadership was severely strained.

Early in school year 2014–15, the principal and two assistant principals met two of the Cultural Proficiency authors and enlisted their support in bringing Cultural Proficiency to the high school. The phase-in process began with a one-day visit to the campus that entailed a four-hour introduction of Cultural Proficiency to a thirty-member core planning group composed of educators, staff members, and community members followed with an end-of-the-day one-hour interactive session with all educators and staff members. All seemed to go well and all members were on good behavior.

Two months later, the core planning group participated in the two-day Tools for Tolerance program held at the Museum of Tolerance in Los Angeles. The two authors leading the Cultural Proficiency work onsite in Santa Maria served as presenter facilitators for the Tools for Tolerance program, too. At the Museum, participants attended sessions and interacted with Terrence Roberts, one of the nine students who desegregated Little Rock High School in 1957, Sylvia Mendez, who in 1946 as an eight-year-old was involved in desegregating an Orange County, California, school, and a gentleman who was a survivor of the Nazi holocaust of the 1930s and 1940s. Between and among these seminars were opportunities for viewing the Museum's venues and for deep dialogue among the core planning group members.

On the second day, and after a particularly powerful mediated presentation, Mr. Galvan, one of the more strident voices at school board meetings, rose to offer a heartfelt apology to the educators in the group. His apology focused on having in the past addressed all educators as a monolithic group. The tension that was in the room when Mr. Galvan first rose to speak flowed from the room. Being one of the two authors working with the high school, I was struck how the room quickly turned on its side. Mr. Galvan was genuinely remorseful for his past comments about educators as a monolithic group. When he concluded his brief remarks, the group sat silent for a few

(Continued)

moments. A few teared up. What followed was an unfiltered dialogue of needing and wanting to move forward in a way that benefitted all students at the school.

The school is on an ascendant trajectory—the spring 2018 graduating class has 83 percent attending institutions of higher education and 67 of the class members from a graduating class of 502 students attending University of California campuses. Yes, problems and communications issues still persist. The gulf between school and community was built over time. Building seamless cooperation between school and community will take time. For me, I am grateful to have been witness to the first step in their journey.

AUTHOR'S ANALYSIS

My first visit to the school, the one-day visit described in the preceding vignette, convinced me of the presence of systemic barriers. However, let me begin with a *climate* observation. In my visit, I was welcomed by all whom I met and was treated in the most congenial manner. I wondered if some folks were a bit surprised that I was a White male. (Over the years I have found my White maleness to be a double-edged sword. On occasion, I have experienced people being relieved I was White and, of course, having *no agenda*; on other occasions I have been challenged with *how could I know what it is like to be a* . . . Most times, though, all goes smoothly.)

Systemic oppression was easy to recognize when examining a historical pattern of student dropout rates, suspension rates, and expulsion rates. When combined with the strained parent/community and school relationships, the sense of privilege and entitlement manifests itself not in intentional acts of defiance by members of the school district but more by their seeming frustration in not knowing how best to respond to voluble criticisms expressed at board meetings where the frequent targets of public comments were district and site administration and the teacher's union. Community members' perceptions of the school's resistance to change were also viewed to be a detached sense of privilege and entitlement.

USING THE FAMILY, SCHOOL, AND COMMUNITY ENGAGEMENT RUBRIC

Being a large school, Santa Maria High School has school members that would be at most every point on the continuum relative to the student population they serve. That said, the school as an organization had prevalent practices that began at Cultural Incapacity and Cultural Blindness and have progressed to Cultural Precompetence and poised to move to Cultural Competence and beyond. The best indicator of Cultural Precompetence was their beginning to know what they didn't know through interacting with members of the *cafecitos* and engaging in deep dialogue like that which occurred during their visit to the Museum of Tolerance. In Chapter 7, an illustration of Cultural Competence is provided.

An Event That Has Never Been Forgotten

I still remember my son Raymundo, a fourth grader, walking into the house after school one afternoon with his gregarious smile and a happy attitude which he has always had, sometimes making it seem that he is not serious about school as I would like him to be. As his babysitter prepared his sister's and his afternoon snack, I asked him, "How was your day, Mijo"? I wanted to know, how was school? What he learned that day? He was not too happy to see me going through his backpack, which was unorganized, with loose papers here and there. I pulled out his graded history chapter test. The test was titled Name and Write the World's Oceans and Continents. For the word "ocean" he wrote Indeon Ocen, Pacifik Ocen, Atlantik Ocen, etc., I thought, great he knows the names of all of the oceans! Then I saw his answers for the continent; North Amerika, Sauth Amerika, Yurope, Azia, Astralia, etc. Once again, I thought great he knows all of his continents! What I failed to notice was the Big Red Circle on top of the page with both a big "F" and a "-0". He had failed his history chapter test! I reread the answers once again and I thought to myself, wait a minute he got all of the answers correct. As I concentrated a bit more, I noticed he had misspelled the answers. He answered and wrote each of the answers the way he had learned how to read.

Prior to coming to this school, he had learned to read through the Whole Language approach in first and second grade. Therefore, he knew the content but did not know how to spell correctly. I thought—was the teacher testing the history chapter test for content or for spelling? If testing for content, it would have been an "A" as he named all of the continents and oceans correctly. If testing for spelling, then it would have been an "F" as he misspelled the words. My inclination as a university professor would have been that he earned a "C," maybe even a higher grade if content was 80 percent and spelling 20 percent!

I later made an appointment to meet with the teacher during the next parent-teacher conference. During that time, I was an assistant professor at a university in the college of education directing the student teaching seminar. We teach teacher candidates to be compassionate yet rigorous in their teaching, we emphasize having rubrics to guide students in their work so they may better explain to parents where their child is and how you go about grading papers. My son's teacher did the opposite. During the meeting with the teacher, I could not convince her to consider grading for both content and spelling. Her response was "By this grade level, they should be able to spell."

AUTHOR'S ANALYSIS

Even after I had provided the teacher with a rationale based on research, and based on my teaching teacher candidates about assessment, she did not want to consider another point of view. I still wonder how many other students received "F's" for not spelling correctly despite knowing the content. How many parents did not meet with her because they were afraid to question authority? How many parents did not meet with her because they were non-English-speaking parents? If she was adamant that her grading policy was a correct one on this assessment and did not want to listen to a university professor with three master's degrees and a doctorate, imagine her attitude with possibly lower income parents and parents with less formal education. The teacher *had education* in terms of an earned degree and teaching credential but as far as I am concerned, her education was lacking. She did not take into account the assets that my son had in this particular instance; he knew the content but needed work on his spelling.

USING THE FAMILY, SCHOOL, AND COMMUNITY ENGAGEMENT RUBRIC

I am sure she did not single out Raymundo for being Latino (culturally destructive) nor did she blame the school system or me for not teaching him how to spell correctly, but she was *culturally blind* by not being able to think beyond the *spelling* as the singular assessment in grading student work.

The School Shooting That Almost Was

The frequency and destructiveness of school shootings in the last few years leaves the sense that our schools are no longer "safe havens for students." School shootings in Santa Fe, Texas; Palmdale, California; and Ocala and Parkland, Florida, have focused the nation's concerned attention on schools. Debates about automatic weapons, bullying, easy access to weapons, and security on campus have resulted in campus protests and school walkouts. This example is derived from one school's experience and how to respond to the situation and the community afterward in the days that follow the shooting scare.

At 8:00 a.m., students were arriving at Riverview School, their local charter K–12 school. Most students were on the school property even though the first class was not in session until 8:25 a.m. Most of the parents and families had dropped their children off at school, left for the day, and were on their way to work or home. At 8:15 a.m., an alert was sent out to families; a lockdown was in place. The email message said for parents to come to the school and get their children or do not bring their children to school if on their way. Families who had been notified or had the chance to read their email rushed to the school only to find that police had set up a perimeter around the school, leaving the parking lot accessible. Families were not allowed to enter the school and students were not released. Family members congregated in the parking lot. No information was provided to the families. No school official was appointed to talk or share information with the family members.

In the school, students were locked in their classrooms with no access to water, food, or bathrooms. In some classes, adults and students were aware that something was going on. Teachers were given limited information. Family members and students

---

could see one another through the windows and started to text or telephone one another. Family members began to ask questions of one another and to police officers who were not at liberty to discuss the situation.

For three more hours, the students remained in the school. The media had arrived by then as they had been contacted by students who were in lockdown at the school. School officials were employing the emergency plan that they developed for use in responding to catastrophic events such as earthquakes, fire drills, etc. Text messages that were continually being sent to parents only served to heighten confusion. In less than an hour, the students were released to family members in a somewhat chaotic manner. Either no procedures were in place or not followed in the dismissal of students. No other communication was sent until later that evening. Family members were left wondering and worrying. Students went home and school administrators debriefed with local police and community leaders.

A week later, family and community members still had not received further information about the active shooter scare/emergency. Many family members asked that a school or community meeting be held to better inform parents and family members of active shooter procedures or revisions of the emergency plan. They wanted to know, for instance, what information could be shared and what couldn't be shared with them. Community members wanted to be more engaged in revising and updating telephone numbers so families could be notified more quickly. They also wanted to actively engage in making the safety plan more accessible in various languages and to create "calling or telephone trees," so families could connect with other families. Parents wondered aloud, what else could they do to help keep their children safe in the event of future threats or lockdowns? They wanted to do their part. School personnel consistently informed family and community members that the school and district "has everything under control." School personnel reiterated all had gone well with the previous threat situation and there was no need for revisions or updates as all the procedures had been followed to the "letter of the law" and that everyone had been kept safe. According to school and district personnel, there was nothing families could add to the process because "we're the experts," "we know what we're doing," and, "besides, no one was hurt."

AUTHOR'S ANALYSIS

Involvement of parents and other community members is fundamental to student safety and success. Schools have crafted policies and police have developed protocols for responding to potential multiple threats at schools. Politicians, police units, teachers, and the communities are engaged in developing policies and plans for potential attacks, but too often, families are not engaged in meaningful ways. By sheer luck, the shooting did not occur. However, this case illustrates how the lack of family and community engagement on issues of this magnitude still has a negative outcome.

Obviously, some facts were not to be shared with parents. For example, the threat had been made by a student who indicated the intent to shoot students in the school. The threat was posted on social media the previous evening and brought to the attention of school authorities the next morning. The particulars of the threat were not made known to the community.

The student who made the threat did not show up at school and did have access to weapons. The police wanted the family members to leave the parking lot because they thought the shooter might start firing on the family members. The school did not have an alternative place for the family members to meet.

After three hours, the lockdown was over and the parents were told that all was well and that their children were safe. Families were encouraged to go about their day as planned and further information would be shared soon through electronic mail or possibly text messages. Families and community members were frantic with fear about their children and were still wondering what had happened and why they weren't told what the threat was and what level of danger their children were in at the school.

USING THE FAMILY, SCHOOL, AND COMMUNITY ENGAGEMENT RUBRIC

If we look at this story and apply the rubric, the behaviors displayed by school leaders are those of cultural blindness on the Cultural Proficiency Continuum. Educator behaviors are characterized by the lack of adapting to the changing needs of parents. In reviewing the rubric for parent engagement, specifically the Essential Element Adapting to Diversity, this school must adapt to the changing landscape of school crisis situations. Riverview, like many schools, has *a* school plan in place to deal with earthquakes, fires, medical emergencies, etc. Most of the plans are detailed and distinctly laid out for staff member and educator use. Emergency plans for earthquakes, fires, and medical emergencies have developed over time and seasoned with the wisdom and experience of experienced administrators. Most plans provide detailed descriptions for the roles of staff, teachers, and administrators.

Family engagement was skimpy and parental input often discouraged. Emergency policies have existed for a number of years in school districts across the country and have proven to be acceptable in the mainstream of public education. Using the rubric, this story illustrates the issues surrounding the Essential Element Managing the Dynamics of Difference defined as the extent to which community involvements develop the capacity to mediate communication and conflict between and among diverse parent/community groups and the school. Historically, issues surrounding emergencies in schools have been handled by school administration. Across the country, the educational climate is shifting toward including parents and family members in an expanding array of school activities; more work is to be done to involve the community in developing and implementing school safety plans.

Across society the last few decades, threat to schools and student safety have become too frequent occurrences. Communication mechanisms at our disposal include internet instruments. Social media instruments such as Twitter, Instagram, and real-time streaming have given families instant communication access to and with schools. Families are now consumers of information related to the school threats and often receive the information at the same time as the school staff and students.

After the incident and in the course of the debriefings at the school, which families strongly advocated for, families were not included until the Parent Action Committee meeting took place later in the month. Although emails were sent to invite families to participate, the information was directive and not necessarily requesting family engagement. When families and schools integrate knowledge about diverse community and organizational cultures into daily practice, we can see that Riverview was at the Cultural Blindness stage. Riverview handled this situation by minimally supporting and sponsoring traditional family and community organizations through relying on the mandated involvement that accompanies federal and state funds, believing those requirements serve all cultural groups.

School culture on issues involving school safety is changing, yet schools are often reluctant to recognize, embrace, and adapt to this new reality. Riverview, with all its progressive thinking and adapting to new curriculum, family, community, and student involvement is fixated on an old pattern of school safety in need of updating.

Reflection

Going Deeper Reflection

Select one or more of the vignettes and think about how you might have reacted to the situation(s). What might be your first or second step in addressing the issue? In thinking of your school or district, what assets do the families and communities served by your school bring to the selected situation? Please use the space below to record your responses.

_____

_____

_____

_____

Going Deeper Dialogic Questions

What engagement opportunities does your school provide for the families and community members served by your school or district? What engagement opportunities does your community provide for your school? What new questions do you want to pose the answers to which might foster better understanding of the diverse cultures served by your school? Please use the space below to record your group's thinking.

_____

_____

_____

_____

SUMMARY

This chapter presented vignettes by the authors regarding their varying experiences with schools. The stories range from personal accounts to experiences too familiar to many families. While these stories are examples of our experiences, they also demonstrate barriers that arise often in schools that align with the first three columns of the Cultural Proficiency Continuum. Sharing our stories about cultural values, race, and school safety are just some of the issues that family and community members can share with schools that can deepen engagement.

LOOKING AHEAD: CHAPTER 7

Chapter 7 presents the more positive experiences and examples of the last three columns of the continuum. Sharing our stories shows that through working collaboratively, systemic and institutional changes can occur in our school communities.

The Guiding Principles Foster Essential Elements as Educator and School Action

Your growth is your business, and it has nothing to do with how anyone else is growing. When you do the best you can, where you are, with what you have, it does not matter what anyone else is doing.

—IYANLA VANZANT, 2001, P. 65

In this chapter, we provide stories of family, school, and community engagement that reflect the core values implicit in the Guiding Principles of Cultural Proficiency. These stories examine the constructive and positive aspects of school community partnering as examples by illustrating use of the Essential Elements of Cultural Competence and Proficiency to guide educator behaviors and the development of school policies and practices. We provide authors' examples extended from the vignettes in Chapter 6 to demonstrate the Essential Elements in action. As you read the stories you may want to refer periodically to Table 1.1, the Family, School, and Community Engagement Rubric located in Chapter 1, and pay particular attention to the intentionality of educator actions and school/district policy pronouncements.

FROM BARRIERS TO CONSTRUCTIVE ACTION

Thankfully, each of the stories/vignettes presented in the preceding chapter has a constructive outcome. As you read each of the entries, reflect on the corresponding story in the previous chapter and, in particular, the barriers that had to be identified and confronted in order for constructive actions to occur.

Individual Actions Lead to Collective Responses

Crestview Hill High School was a new school that had only been open a few years when my daughter Angelique attended. The school had an ethnically and linguistically diverse population of about 2,000 students. Many were on free and reduced lunch and came from the rural outskirts of town. Even as a new school, it was robust in its after-school activities, sports, and academics. The principal had recruited teachers from other schools in the district as well as teachers from other districts.

One day, in Mr. Martin's tenth grade chemistry classroom, students busily chatted in groups of four about the day's topics and assignments. Angelique, a soft-spoken,

(Continued)

(Continued)

bright young lady, was often required to work with others in groups. Mostly an intro-vert, she preferred working alone to complete projects rather than to work in groups. Greg, an African American male, was talkative and outspoken in class. Greg was larger and heavier than most of the students in tenth grade—someone that might consider him "big-boned" for his age. To get started, they had begun discussing their topic, researching it, and writing their answers to the questions for their group project. As the groups in the classroom discussed their projects, Greg continued to use "the N word" in his dialogue with Angelique and his classmates. As Greg kept talking, he was also getting out of his seat and talking with other members of the class looking for ideas. Although he wasn't always addressing Angelique directly, she was very uncomfort-able with him using "the N word" during their discussions. She asked him a few times to stop saying the word. He would stop for a while but soon he would revert back to using the word throughout the class period. She didn't know how to respond since other students were saying and using the word while the teacher walked around the classroom monitoring students' progress. She was certain Greg and the other students were speaking loud enough for the teacher to hear their voices.

The next week, Angelique talked with me about what happened in class and how Greg's constant use of "the N word" was just "getting on her nerves." She sounded exasperated. She was beginning to dislike chemistry. I encouraged her to speak with her teacher, Mr. Martin, and let him know so that he could be informed about the lan-guage that was being used in class, in case he hadn't heard it spoken in class. She said she had already mentioned it to him earlier in the week, but Mr. Martin didn't think it was a big deal, since "a lot of the Black kids talk like that."

At first, Angelique was apprehensive about me approaching Mr. Martin but soon decided that it was her best recourse. She noticed that Greg not only used "the N word," but often cursed in class. She also knew that he had already been in two fights that year. I encouraged Angelique to speak with Mr. Martin again, but she was becoming too anx-ious and nervous about the situation, and feared that Greg would find out that she had spoken to Mr. Martin. Angelique and I continued to discuss the best way to approach this situation, and finally decided that I should have a conversation with Mr. Martin.

I sent Mr. Martin an email and explained the situation to him, and how this was emo-tionally and physically affecting Angelique and her attitude about coming to his class. I asked him to call me at his earliest convenience. Mr. Martin called me during his prep period the very next day. I told him about my conversation with Angelique and how uncomfortable she had felt working with and being around Greg. After our discussion, Mr. Martin's responsive action was the following:

1. Mr. Martin admitted that he'd heard Greg and some of the other African American students use the word in class many times, but thought that since the students using "the N word" were African American, it was alright.

2. Mr. Martin separated Angelique and Greg from the original group and put them individually with other separate groups;

3. Mr. Martin stated that he would listen more intently to the conversations and language that were being used in his classroom and address the issue immediately whenever "the N word" was being used;

4. Mr. Martin said that he appreciated the telephone call and the information that I had shared about the history of the word, its implications, and its negative impact on both African American and non-African American students;

5. Mr. Martin also said that he would make an extra effort to "watch out" for Angelique to ensure she felt comfortable in his class so that she could have the best experience in learning chemistry.

6. This incident was later brought up at a faculty/staff meeting and the leadership team decided to address it immediately. Mr. Martin took the information, reflected on it, and realized that he was a part of the problem. He had been allowing and "approving" the behavior to continue to occur by his silence and by not addressing it. This situation happens too frequently in schools where students are using inappropriate language and teachers ignore it or don't know how to handle it.

ESSENTIAL ELEMENTS

Several of the Essential Elements are applicable to this story; our focus is on Institutionalizing Cultural Knowledge. The Essential Element Institutionalizing Cultural Knowledge serves to shift what we're doing now to how individuals can make personal change and can initiate institutional, systemic change. By expressing his concern for what was occurring in his classroom, Mr. Martin brought the subject of appropriate language to the attention of the entire faculty. He wasn't the only teacher or staff member who had brought up *racially relevant* issues.

Several situations occurred on campus that many teachers and staff of color and their White allies viewed as insensitive, racist, unwelcoming, and unbecoming of a newly formed school that had made very public a shared vision of making a positive impact on academic achievement and learning for all students. Earlier in the school year, swastikas were found painted on the walls of the boys' restrooms. A few weeks later, according to eyewitnesses, three White young men started a fight with an African American young man. Although all were fighting, only the African American student was suspended, even though it was his first fight; the others were given detention.

A few of the teachers were aware of my having been escorted from a classroom by school security officers the previous year (see Chapter 6). As some caring teachers apologized and expressed to me after that incident, "Why would a principal arrange for a parent who comes to campus to visit a classroom be escorted out by security—in front of students and in front of your daughter? What kind of principal does that?"

Many were fed up with the nonactions, complacency, and passive-aggressive behavior of the White principal with regard to racially charged incidents on campus. It was widely assumed that the principal's focus was on pleasing the *older White guard* at the district office and being promoted to a district-level position someday. To avert a complete mutiny, the respected non-formal leaders of the school spoke passionately about taking action and the principal relented. These non-formal leaders knew that these incidents were not solely *Black issues* or something that Black students were going to have to handle on their own. This series of events became an equity issue for the entire school to address.

First, this emergent leadership team contacted The Village Nation, an advocacy group composed of three African American male teachers, who had been successful working with African American students at their school in Southern California. The emergent leadership team discussed hosting grade-level assemblies to talk about racial issues and the use of "the N word" on campus. This idea was quickly challenged. African American teachers and staff at Crestview Hill thought that an assembly with just the African American students should be held prior to including the entire student body. They wanted to give a historical context to "the N word" and how it had been used for centuries to demean and dehumanize African Americans. Teaching about the origins of stereotypes and prejudices represented another aspect of educators using the Essential Element Institutionalizing Cultural Knowledge. The African American faculty and staff felt strongly that the initial assembly should have only African American faculty, staff, and students present to discuss the issues openly, to have "real talk." The faculty and staff respected their African American colleagues' point of view and agreed to the strategy.

African American parents, staff, community members, and clergy were invited to the assembly to support one another and to learn from each other. With pressure from the faculty and staff, the catalyst for change began by introducing and using the Essential Element Institutionalizing Cultural Knowledge with the African American students and led by the African American teachers and staff and African American family and community members. The second successful illustration of Institutionalizing Cultural Knowledge was the incorporation of the historical and current effects of dehumanizing language into the learning of the students, faculty, and staff members of the school.

Leading From the Strawberry Fields, Santa Maria, California[1]

As indicated in Chapter 6, the school is on an ascendant trajectory. A vignette or story that exemplifies school community engagement is what is known as *Leading From the Strawberry Fields*, which was published as an article in *Leadership*, the journal of the Association of California School Administrators.

On leaving that remarkable meeting at the Museum of Tolerance, I felt confident that progress in school community communication was at hand. I had no idea of the form it was to take just a few months later. The story is best told from the voices of two educators who served as assistant principal and principal at the time and who

---

[1]A PDF copy of the article *Leading From the Strawberry Fields* is available at the website for The Center for Culturally Proficient Educational Practice: www.ccpep.org. At the website, locate the button, "Articles" and then proceed to locate and download the article. The article appeared in the January/February 2017 issue of *Leadership*, a publication of the Association of California School Administrators.

are leading change efforts at the high school, Peter Flores III, assistant principal, and Joseph Domingues, principal:

> Goal No. 2 of the Santa Maria Joint Union High School District's Local Control and Accountability Plan speaks specifically to the issues of Cultural Proficiency and parent engagement. "Using supplemental and concentration funding, our district is working to 'create a culture of respect and caring that supports positive relationships among stakeholders' as identified in our goal," said Santa Maria JUHSD Superintendent Mark Richardson.
>
> Parents, community members, and educators from across the Santa Maria community have been engaged in school-community talks focused on recent increases in gang-related violence plaguing the community. Santa Maria High School, Santa Maria Joint Union High School District, and Santa Maria Bonita School District in partnership with the Santa Maria Police Department recently took the advice of one community member that led to an unintended positive consequence.
>
> Working with Mr. Romero, who is a sergeant in the Santa Maria Police Department, two educators from the Santa Maria-Bonita School District (an elementary school district that feeds into the high school district), two administrators from the Santa Maria Joint Union High School District, and Mr. Romero made arrangements for a parent meeting during the lunch break of the workers at a local strawberry field.
>
> . . .
>
> We made our journey to the strawberry field with high hopes and experienced an unintended and very positive consequence. During the time we were conducting the parent meeting the grower/owner joined our meeting and expressed that he could see value in this type of parent participation and invited us to return.
>
> Growers/owners made a commitment to give parents paid release time to visit their children's schools. The conversations that took place with parents were authentic and we learned more about them personally. We felt that we, the educators, gained mutual respect from the visit—from both the parents and the growers/owners.
>
> Once we concluded our "school meeting," the parents gave us a tour of their work area and tasks. The parents demonstrated a sense of pride showing us the complexities and care of their hard work.
>
> **Lessons Learned**
>
> Our objective in "taking the school to the community" was to more directly engage parents with their children's education. We were able to inform the parents about the need to have them involved in helping us stop gang-related activity within the community. We were helping build bridges for stemming violence and at the same time surface some of our own falsely held assumptions about youth gang members. Migrant workers are willing to be our partners to protect and serve their communities and help educate their children and families.

(Continued)

(Continued)

We knew this was only the first step in what might be a long journey. It has become more than a "first step." It becomes many steps for us as school leaders in recognizing and valuing the diversity of our community. As importantly, we developed deep appreciation for this inside/out, interactive role of field workers and growers/owners and the manner in which both are important constituencies of our schools. Finally, and maybe most importantly, we have a deeper understanding of ourselves as school leaders in working across constituencies in supporting equitable educational opportunities for our students, their children.

So, we ask you, Where are your Strawberry Fields? Who else do you engage with in your community to better serve your students? Transformative leadership takes you into the community and requires you to ask questions about who is being well served by the school and district and who needs to be served better or differently. What will it take for you to discover your Strawberry Fields?

Source: Flores III, Peter and Domingues, Joseph (2017). *Leading from the Strawberry Fields: Transformative Leadership in Santa Maria.* Association of California School Administrators, Leadership Magazine, January/February issue. Reprinted with permission.

ESSENTIAL ELEMENTS

There is evidence of each of the Essential Elements in the Santa Maria vignette and for our purposes in this chapter we highlight the Essential Element Managing the Dynamics of Difference. *Managing* and *difference* connote the potential for conflict if not the outright existence of personal and/or intergroup conflict. This element holds that conflict is natural and normal. Conflict between and among individuals let alone groups of individuals will occur. When potential conflict can be approached as an opportunity to engage with others in search of mutually satisfying desired outcomes, it provides opportunities for *win–win* outcomes. Mr. Romero approached the school and the grower's supervisor in search of opportunities for parents' voices to be heard. The school districts and their partners in the local police department were willing to hold the meeting at a time and place convenient to the workers. Unanticipated in this vignette was the unannounced appearance of the owner who immediately saw the benefit in having workers' family needs met. For school members, the community expanded to include the workers in meaningful conversation and expanded to include the owner and his support for the workers.

From Event Never Forgotten to Inclusive College Professor

My son is now a community college professor teaching a history course, Chicano and Cross-cultural Studies. He makes sure to give credit to students who know the content he is teaching as well as asking for improvement when students misspell words or have grammatical errors in their essays. He teaches from a culturally proficient perspective by embracing his students' cultures as assets and works to improve their academic success by implementing the five essential elements in his teaching process.

Mundo practices the Essential Elements by acknowledging who is in his classes, from young adults to reentry students. He Values the Diversity of different cultural groups of students from Latinxs, Iraqis, African Americans, LGTBQ students, athletes, and others. He Manages the Dynamics of Difference occasioned by having a diverse student population by using multiple forms of assessment. How do I know this? I co-taught a Cultural Proficiency course with my son during the Spring 2018 semester where I witnessed and experienced his efforts in promoting and supporting culturally proficient practices. Mundo's learning about issues of community engagement began in his fourth grade classroom. It was in that fourth grade classroom experience that he began the development of an awareness of inclusivity, whether expressly aware of it or not. His community grounding was so strong that he developed a *both-and* perspective that serves him well as an educator today.

Takeaways From a Shooting That Almost Was

Riverview School leads the way in school innovation and parent involvement. As a public charter school, serving the needs of all students serves as the solid foundation for this school. From the beginning parent involvement was instrumental in building the school as a community creating and supporting an inclusive and safe environment for students, staff, and teachers. This school is unique in the way that they have involved parents in every aspect of their child's school experiences. Families have direct access to teachers, school directors, and staff on a daily basis. Families do more than volunteer; they have been involved in direct service delivery to their students.

One child, who was starting kindergarten at Riverview, was identified as special needs and was entitled to a full-time aide. The school and the district were in agreement and developed an Individual Education Plan (IEP) and the plan was put into place. The IEP meeting was held with all the appropriate personnel present. Educational and wraparound services were offered and everyone agreed, including the parents. A special education aide was hired who would be one-to-one with the child every day. In the course of the conversation, an invitation was extended to the parent to be a part of the education aide interview panel. The district responded by insisting that this has never been done. It wasn't part of the standard protocol and district personnel believed that involving the parent was giving the parent and child wrong messages about areas of responsibility. The district made it clear that they were in charge and would screen and hire the aide without parental involvement. At this point, the Riverview administrator of special education spoke up and defended the decision to allow the parent to be part of the process. "We believe that parents should be involved in all aspects of their child's education. We believe in collaboration, communication, and building the process together."

The Family, School, and Community Engagement Rubric can be used to assess Riverview's commitment to the Essential Elements of Cultural Competence/Proficiency with particular focus on Valuing Diversity and Assessing Cultural Knowledge. Valuing Diversity is evident in the way district personnel responded to the parent and how parents previously had been excluded from a most important process in this school. Riverview took immediate corrective action. Acknowledging families from the first time they walk onto a school's campus to involving them in key decisions exhibits a culture of welcoming and valuing parents. Being acknowledged and respected is foundational to caring and collaboration.

Assessing Cultural Knowledge was demonstrated by the extent to which community involvement facilitated the identification, assessment, and development of cultural identity of this student's special need. Riverview's inclusive practices are located well within Cultural Competence on the Continuum. Family, school, and community leaders learn about each other's cultures in order to bridge the gaps between and among home, community, and school cultures. Involving families in the selection of the special education aide dramatically affected the student success and family interactions. For ten years, Riverview and the parent have remained partners in the successful educational experience for this student.

Reflection

In considering any or all of these vignettes, what is important for you to capture in note form right now—your thoughts, your feelings, your questions? How might you respond to the question at the end of the last vignette—*What will it take for you to discover your Strawberry Fields?* Please use the space below to record your thinking.

_____

_____

_____

_____

Going Deeper Reflection

Each of the vignettes in Chapter 6 amplified core values that embraced others' cultures as deficits and Chapter 7 amplified underlying core values that held cultures as an asset on which to build educational experiences. From these two chapters, what are you learning, or affirming, about having core values that are overtly inclusive of other cultures? What are you learning, or affirming, about educators and their schools making equity and inclusivity known to all? Please use the space below to record your responses.

_____

_____

_____

_____

Going Deeper Dialogic Questions

In your learning communities or grade level/department meetings, in what ways do parents and community members know your institutional core values? What do you want to learn about the cultural communities that arrive at your school? In what ways might you integrate any new learning into your espoused values and your school's actions? Please use the space below to record your and your group's initial thinking.

_____

_____

_____

_____

SUMMARY

The authors' stories shared here give hope and clarity to families and schools working together to resolve issues. Many issues such as the ones shared here happen too often without adequate and appropriate responses. Our purpose is to illustrate possible positive outcomes when the Essential Elements are practiced and when policies are constructed to support culturally proficient engagement.

LOOKING AHEAD: CHAPTER 8

Chapter 8 presents a template that can be used two ways: (1) to develop a plan of family, school, and community engagement; or (2) to assess your current plan of action and to make changes deemed appropriate. You have already completed the first and most crucial step in deep, authentic family and community engagement. By getting to this point in the book you have demonstrated commitment. From here it is all downhill! Now that you recognize the need and/or you have the desire, we will help guide you to develop the goal and the attendant steps along the way.

PART IV

Commit to Action

The 8th C—Commit to Action

You have to run your own race. Run it like a marathon. And just steadily build energy for yourself so that when you're on the last lap, you're stronger than ever.

—OPRAH WINFREY, JUNE 2011, P. 157

Inspiration and motivation for writing this book come from the many interactions we have with our PreK–12 educator colleagues who often ask, "This Cultural Proficiency approach all sounds well and good, but how do we get families involved? How do we get started? What can we do to get families to come to school?"

In getting to this point in the book, you have reflected on your professional experiences as an educator, your personal experiences as and with family and community members, and the work with your educator colleagues. You are prepared now to embark on a Cultural Proficiency journey with colleagues to engage the communities served by your school or district in new and effective ways. You are ready to commit to action.

This chapter is designed to support your planning and your execution of the plan. We present concepts for your consideration in planning, initiating, and increasing engagement with the diverse communities served by your school or district.

The first section of this chapter serves as a primer for contrasting traditional strategies with inclusive strategies for initiating and guiding culturally proficient engagement practices. The second part of the chapter presents self-assessments. The assessments emphasize the inside-out approach to family and community engagement that have you check your assumptions with regard to your community. Before proceeding, it is important to take note that assessment is *not* evaluation. As you proceed with your planning, assessments are used to note where you are in planning and execution of plan for the purpose of making appropriate and necessary adjustments.

The third section is the *biggie*—planning to plan. Yes, that is the correct phrase—*planning to plan*. In planning to plan, you will use the resources from this book and bring them together to complete the planning guide.

Being an advocate for family and community capacity creates an inclusive environment for educators with the family and community members served by the school or district. Educators advocating for community members' support for a school demonstrates commitment to mutual growth and learning among educators and community members. Take a moment to read and study Table 8.1, which contrasts traditional strategies to attract and recruit family members with inclusive relationship building and technologically appropriate strategies. Notice how the information shifts from informing to inclusive practice.

TABLE 8.1

Traditional and Culturally Proficient Family, School, and Community Engagement Capacity Building Strategies

Traditional Parent Involvement	Culturally Proficient Family, School, and Community Engagement Capacity Building Strategies
Phase I (Introduction)	**Phase I (Introduction)**
Invitation to individuals	Invitation to groups or teams
Communication with parent through flyers/print	Communication with family using electronic mail, social media, text messaging, and group messages in several languages
Communication regarding student usually negative (first)	Communication regarding student positive (first)
Phase II (Meeting)	**Phase II (Meeting)**
Meeting agenda set by school personnel	Meeting agenda set by group or team; includes input from family/community
Parent sessions determined by school personnel	Family sessions structured and set with working families in mind
	Interpreters
Parent/teacher conferences after school	Family/teacher conferences throughout day to accommodate parent/family
Parent/teacher lived in/near community	Home-school visit by teacher, administrator, school personnel
Phase III (Retaining)	**Phase III (Retaining)**
Content of meetings focused on what parent should do	Content focused on how school and families work together for student success
Content of meetings focused on curricular standards	Content of meetings focus on goals for children and youth

Reflection

Take another minute or two and reread Table 8.1. In what ways are the actions in the two columns different? Please use the space below to record your observations.

_____

_____

_____

_____

USING PRE-ASSESSMENTS TO GET STARTED

The Family, School, and Community Self-Assessment (Figure 8.1) is a tool to guide personal and institutional change. Here are pre-assessments that can be used as resources:

- Parent-Teacher Association's National Standards for Family-School Partnerships Assessment Guide (www.pta.org/files/National_Standards_ Assessment_Guide.pdf)

- California Department of Education's and WestEd's Family Engagement Framework (www.wested.org/wp-content/files_mf/1414600912familyenga gementframework2.pdf)

- Families in Schools' Ready or Not Report (www.familiesinschools.org/ ready-or-not-parent-engagement-in-california-lcff/).

We suggest using these assessments to establish baseline readiness and openness for change and action. As you and your colleagues reflect on how you responded to the prompts, Figure 8.1 provides you and each educator a beginning point of discussions for your school team as you develop your plan to initiate and deepen your work with students, families, and communities. Carefully note areas of agreement as well as areas of divergent perspectives. Thoughtful discussions about your candid responses to The Family and Community Self-Assessment can be a useful guide in your progress toward cultural outreach and inclusivity. As areas of commonality emerge, identify areas of strength and areas of difference. Strength areas provide the bases for growth and areas of difference reveal where increased work is to be focused.

FIGURE 8.1

Family, School, and Community Engagement Self-Assessment

Please rate your school or district in the following areas:

1. Recognizes that all parents, regardless of income, educational level, or cultural background, want their children to do well in school and are involved in their children's learning.

1	2	3	4
rarely	sometimes	regularly	always

2. Creates policies and programs that will support families to guide their children's learning.

1	2	3	4
rarely	sometimes	regularly	always

3. Works with families to build their social and political connections.

1	2	3	4
rarely	sometimes	regularly	always

4. Develops the capacity of school staff to work with families.

1	2	3	4
rarely	sometimes	regularly	always

5. Links family and community engagement efforts to student learning.

1	2	3	4
rarely	sometimes	regularly	always

6. Focuses efforts to engage families on developing trust and respect.

1	2	3	4
rarely	sometimes	regularly	always

7. Embraces a philosophy of partnership and shares power with families and communities.

1	2	3	4
rarely	sometimes	regularly	always

8. Builds strong connections between schools and community organizations.

1	2	3	4
rarely	sometimes	regularly	always

Source: Ferguson, C., Jordan, C., Wood, L., Rodriguez, V., & Buttram, J. (2005). *Beyond the building: A facilitation guide for school family and community connections*, p. 27. Austin, TX: Southwest Educational Development Laboratory.

The most effective use of the instrument is for participants to complete theirs individually. Once each participant has had an opportunity to think about and record their responses, they are well prepared to engage in sharing responses, the act of which means in deep dialogue and for shared understanding to emerge. Dialogue and shared understanding are indicators of educators' readiness and willingness to engage communities in authentic ways. Dialogic discussions among faculty and staff members can lead to developing shared core values that serve to guide community engagement efforts.

Once the members in your organization understand where they are and agree to a level of intentional equity and a commitment to change, action-oriented steps can be taken to recruit families and community members, welcome them, and sustain high levels of engagement. With this awareness and commitment to community engagement, you and your team help and encourage each other through this process.

In Chapter 5, we presented the 7 Cs as skills and knowledge-based concepts for you to consider as you're building capacity for family and community engagement. The 7 Cs' approaches are intended to promote high-quality, equity-focused programs, policies, and practices.

PLANNING TO PLAN

The temptation for you right now might be to jump right to Figure 8.2 and begin developing your action plan, related strategies, and assessment measures. We certainly understand the motivation for doing so, but implore you to take a few preliminary steps by summarizing what you and your colleagues have learned from your reading thus far and ensuring that concepts of equity and inclusivity are intentionally woven into your family and community engagement plan. A preliminary step is to take some time to complete and review the Participant Perception of School or District Relative to Cultural Proficiency's Essential Elements (Table 8.2) chart.

If you are working as a leadership team, we recommend that each member complete this section individually and then discuss your responses. Engaging in dialogue increases mutual respect and cross-cultural understanding, and promotes shared commitment to actions.

TABLE 8.2

Participant Perception of School or District Relative to District's Cultural Proficiency's Essential Elements

	Cultural Destructiveness	Cultural Incapacity	Cultural Blindness	Cultural Precompetence	Cultural Competence	Cultural Proficiency
Assessing Cultural Knowledge						
Valuing Diversity						
Managing Dynamics of Difference						
Adapting to Diversity						
Institutionalizing Cultural Knowledge						

online resources 🔲   Available for download at **resources.corwin.com/CPPartnership**

The 7 Cs. Turning your attention for a few moments back to Chapter 5, in what ways do your school's interactions with families and community members currently practice each C and, then, in what ways do you think growth could be promoted?

- Collaboration
  - Current practice:
  - An area of growth potential:
- Communication
  - Current practice:
  - An area of growth potential:
- Caring
  - Current practice:
  - An area of growth potential:
- Culture
  - Current practice:
  - An area of growth potential:
- Community
  - Current practice:
  - An area of growth potential:
- Connectedness
  - Current practice:
  - An area of growth potential:
- Collective Responsibility
  - Current practice:
  - An area of growth potential:

FROM NEGATIVE TO CONSTRUCTIVE

Chapter 6 provided school-based illustrations of *negatives* in terms of barriers to be overcome in planning and executing an inclusive and equitable plan for family and community engagement. In marked contrast, Chapter 7 provided school-based descriptions of *positives* that flow from guiding principles that serve as core values that foster and reinforce equity and inclusion.

The Family and Community Engagement Rubric in Chapter 1 is a device that illustrates both negative and constructive engagement. Take a few moments and return to the Rubric on pages 16–17 and, individually and without consulting colleagues, indicate where you see this school or this district along the Continuum for each of the Essential Elements.

An important next step is for your planning group to share your observations from Table 8.2. Listen to one another. Resist trying to talk others into changing their views. Listen to understand, not to refute. Do not attempt to reach consensus. Only attempt to hear and to be heard. Thoughtful sharing and dialogue provide rich information for finding common ground as you bring the diversity of participants' backgrounds and experiences to the planning.

YOUR CULTURAL PROFICIENCY FAMILY, SCHOOL, AND COMMUNITY ENGAGEMENT ACTION PLAN

The Cultural Proficiency Family, School, and Community Engagement Action Plan (Figure 8.2) is presented as your next step. As a part of this next phase, you may want to browse through the list of learning strategies presented in Chapter 9. Some familiar learning strategies are presented for your team to consider while you're completing the Action Plan.

The Action Plan format continues to evolve in our books. The version in this book is adapted from Lindsey, Thousand, Jew, and Piowlski (2018), *Culturally Proficient Inclusive Schools: All Means All!* The version in this chapter is also consistent with the version used by the Center for Culturally Proficient Educational Practice (www.ccpep.org).

The Cultural Proficiency Family, School, and Community Engagement Action Plan is derived from the Complex Change Action Planning approach (Lindsey, Thousand, Jew, & Piowlski, 2018; Villa & Thousand, 2017; Villa, Thousand, & Nevin, 2013). This action plan brings together concepts from this book for you to use together with variables of complex change to create and sustain a Culturally Proficient Family, School, and Community Engagement Action Plan.

Figure 8.2 provides the Culturally Proficient Family, School, and Community Engagement Action Plan as a template to help guide your thinking and planning. The template is to guide your consideration of key actions as you plan to address four variables of vision, skills, incentives, and resources that must be considered for a complex change for family, school, and community engagement to occur and be lasting.

COMPONENTS OF A CULTURALLY PROFICIENT FAMILY, SCHOOL, AND COMMUNITY ENGAGEMENT PLAN

The Culturally Proficient Family, School, and Community Engagement Plan includes components familiar to most educator planning mechanisms. *School Vision and Mission Statements*—The goals and actions outlined in the Action Plan are to align with the school's shared vision and mission. For each goal, those developing the Action Plan must ask the question, "To what extent does this goal align with the current vision and mission statements?" If it is determined that the goal and the vision and mission statements align, all is well, and the next steps of determining actions to achieve the goal are generated. If it is desired that a proposed goal to forward culturally proficient family engagement does not appear to align with the vision or mission, the goal may be reconsidered or reshaped. Or a different question may be asked, namely, "Do the school's vision and mission statements

FIGURE 8.2

The Culturally Proficient Family, School, and Community Engagement Action Plan

School Community:					
Our School Vision:					
Our School Mission:					

Goals by Change Variable	Culturally Proficient Actions	Success Measure(s) *"We will know we are successful if/when . . ."*	Person(s) Responsible:	Date by Which to be Achieved:	Actual Outcomes:

• What goals do we need to address and achieve each variable?
 	
• Is the goal written using SMART criteria?
 	
• To what extent does the goal align with current vision and mission statements? Do the vision and/or mission statements need to be revisited or revised to better align with Culturally Proficient Inclusive values?
	• List actions chronologically
	
	• Include preparation (e.g., funding) and implementation actions
	
	• Include actions for
	  ☐ Assessing Cultural Knowledge and the current reality
	  ☐ Valuing Diversity
	  ☐ Managing the Dynamics of Diversity
	  ☐ Adapting to Diversity
	  ☐ Institutionalizing Cultural Knowledge
		• What is measured?
		• Who will measure?
		• When to measure?			

VISION: Developing and Sustaining Family and Community Engagement					
What goals do we need to reach this outcome?					
Goal One:	Actions to Achieve Goal One:	Success Measure(s):	Person(s) Responsible:	Date:	Outcomes:
Goal Two:	Actions to Achieve Goal Two:	Success Measure(s):	Person(s) Responsible:	Date:	Outcomes:

Adapted from *A Guide to Co-teaching: Practical Tips for Facilitating Student Learning*, 3rd ed., by Richard A. Villa, Jacqueline S. Thousand, and Ann I. Nevin. Thousand Oaks, CA: Corwin, www.corwin.com.

online resources 🔽 Available for download at **resources.corwin.com/CPPartnership** need to be reexamined and updated to reflect cultural changes and advancements in best educational practice?" As times and culture change, so must school vision and mission statements. Culturally proficient learning communities revisit vision and mission statements on regular bases and, if necessary, revise and refine the statements to align with the contemporary values of the community.

Goals. The Action Plan is designed to grow and support educators to consider and implement new strategies for ensuring family and community engagement opportunities for cultural sectors of the community. The planning team determines outcomes needed to address complex change variables (i.e., vision, skills, incentives, and resources) and translates them into observable and measurable goals for which specific action steps can be formulated. As shown in Figure 8.2, team members are prompted to answer the question, "What goals do we need to reach these outcomes?" for the outcomes of

- instilling and installing a *vision* of inclusive family, school, and community engagement,

- building *skills* and capacity for culturally proficient family, school, and community engagement,

- providing *incentives* to engage community members in culturally proficient inclusive family and community engagement practices, and

- orchestrating technical, material, organizational, and human *resources* for family and community engagement.

We recommend action planners compose SMART goals. SMART is an acronym for the following five attributes of a quality goal.

Specific = The goal identifies the who, what, when, where, which, and why of the goal.

Measurable = The goal includes concrete criteria (e.g., how much, how many, how we will know) for measuring success.

Attainable = The goal considers what is needed (e.g., development of people's knowledge, skills, attitudes, and resources) to make the goal achievable.

Realistic = The crafters of the goal answer "yes" to two questions: "Is the goal high enough?" and "Are we willing to work hard enough to reach it?"

Timely and **T**angible = The crafters of the goal answer "yes" to the following questions: "Do we have a sense of urgency? Do we have a timeline with short- and long-term actions to achieve the goal? Can we picture the outcome? Do we know when we have reached the goal? (Lindsey, Nuri-Robins, Terrell, & Lindsey, 2018, pp. 163–164; Lawlor & Hornyak, 2012, pp. 259–267; Morrison, 2010)

FIGURE 8.3

Example of a SMART goal for Engagement and Partnership

Specific—Our Family and School Partnership Coalition (FSPC) wants to increase our family engagement outreach efforts to build meaningful relationships between families and schools. To extend our efforts, home visits will begin this September with two of our middle schools to initiate and establish contact between families and school personnel. Participants in the home visits will be asked to complete a survey to assess the impact of the visits.

Measurable—Based on last year's family survey results, our goals are to increase home visits by 15 percent, with a 50 percent increase in the number of visits with emergent bilingual families. We will make approximately ten to fifteen additional home visits by December to learn and observe how families help their child(ren) and youth at home. Each one-hour-long visit will consist of a team of two trained teachers.

Attainable—To achieve this goal, several steps need to be taken. We need to ask teachers at the beginning of school for volunteers to be trained on the home-visit process. Families who have already volunteered to be part of the process will be visited before December of this year; others will be scheduled for visits after January of next year. Since the proposal has already been written and approved, but is still fairly new to the district, the findings from last year will be included in the presentation to the board no later than the district's September meeting.

Realistic—One of our FSPC goals is to increase family engagement at the middle schools in the district. We were able to get helpful suggestions from our Family and Neighborhood Connections Facebook pages, our Engagement Coordinator Twitter account, and last year's participants. Home visits are a relevant partnership-building strategy that has funding supported by the district and the regional teacher association. To prepare for this year's visits, there is a compiled list of volunteer families and a pool of trained teachers ready to participate from which to choose.

Timeline or Tangible—August 2020–May 2021.

In this example (Figure 8.3), the focus is on building capacity through home visits in the community's middle schools. The number of families to be visited is clearly stated, when they are to be visited, how long the visits should take, and who should go. Measuring the impact of those visits will provide data for continuous planning and commitment.

- **Culturally Proficient Actions.** In Figure 8.2, the Family, School, and Community Engagement Action Plan, culturally proficient actions are listed in the second column. Action steps are carefully planned, chronologically ordered behaviors that help move a team toward achieving their goals in each of the complex change dimensions of vision, skills, incentives, and resources. Both preparation and implementation actions should be included in an action sequence. Planned actions are built on the 5 Essential Elements of Cultural Proficiency (noted at the top of the second column) and best practices for organizational transformation along the dimensions of complex change. For demonstrated concrete actions for building vision, skills, incentives, and resources, see Villa and Thousand (2017) and Villa, Thousand, and Nevin (2013). The action steps are the heart of the success of the Action Plan.

- **Accountability and Measures of Success.** Goals need to be measurable so you and your team can benchmark (measure how you are doing at any point in time) your actions for points of success or *stuckness*. Benchmarking is a leadership action that helps a team move forward based upon data rather than wonder how they are doing or assume the results are good or bad. In the third column of the Figure 8.2 action plan, see the starter phrase "*We will know we are successful if/when . . .*". This is the phrase you and your teammates must next contemplate, discuss, and agree upon, remembering that success measures, data, and benchmarks must be observable and measurable. *What* is measured? What *are* the measures? What data will you collect? What are benchmarking questions for tracking progress toward achieving the SMART goals (identified in the plan's first column) and implementing the *actions* (identified in the plan's second column)? *Who* will be responsible for collecting and examining data and benchmarks? *When* or how often will data and benchmarks be examined to assess progress? The results of analyzing these data are fed back into the plan in ways to support continuous learning. The plan itself may be revised as your team analyzes data. The fourth and fifth columns of Figure 8.2 identify *who* will provide oversight of actions and goals and the *date* by which a goal or action is to be accomplished.

- **Actual Outcomes.** The last and sixth column of our Figure 8.2 Family, School, and Community Engagement Action Plan provides a place to note *actual outcomes*. Planned outcomes are not always what people think they will be. Sometimes outcomes fall short of what was hoped for; sometimes they surprise and exceed expectations; and sometimes they just are different than what was expected, but just as good or even better!

Review Figure 8.2 and think about how to apply the actual outcomes to your school and district. In what ways might this action plan template support your planning for a culturally proficient inclusive education environment? (Lindsey, Thousand, Jew, & Piowlski, 2018).

Reflection

What have you learned or affirmed in your thinking about the value of developing an action plan? What are you feeling? What concerns, if any, do you have? In what ways does the planning template inform your and your school's work? In what ways do the 5 Essential Elements of Cultural Proficiency inform your work?

_____

_____

_____

_____

SUMMARY

This chapter presented the planning stages in three parts: Comparing traditional capacity building strategies with culturally proficient strategies; using pre-assessments to establish a foundation of where you and your institution are; and third, how to use and complete the Family, School, and Community Engagement Action Plan.

LOOKING AHEAD: CHAPTER 9

Chapter 9 describes familiar learning strategies to engage families and communities. There are levels of resources that can be adapted in various forms to build dual capacity and continue to fashion the Essential Elements of Cultural Proficiency as action strategies that deepen community inclusivity at your school or district—which results in greater access and success for students from all cultural groups.

Resources

CULTURALLY PROFICIENT PLANNING FOR INCLUSIVE PARTNERING AND CAPACITY BUILDING

Every person in the world is a learner. From the cradle to the grave we are continually learning the lessons of life.

—REV. JESSE EMANUEL CLARK, MAY 10, 1970, P. 1

Educators who are engaged with families and communities can be partners and co-creators of inclusive and equitable educational experiences for their children and youth. As mentioned in Chapter 1, the difference between parent involvement and family engagement speaks to the depth of interactions. As such, programs that focus on one or the other often have different purposes, goals, and outcomes. Culturally proficient community engagement ensures the focus of capacity building is on culturally inclusive engagement, as well as on valuing and building culturally inclusive relationships with all sectors of the community served by the school. Larry Ferlazzo, the coauthor of *Building Parent Engagement in Schools* (Ferlazzo & Hammond, 2009), summarizes well what we intend with culturally proficient engagement, with our added caveat of being intentional in ensuring inclusive outreach efforts and results:

> A school striving for **family involvement** often leads with its mouth—identifying projects, needs, and goals and then telling parents how they can contribute. A school striving for **parent engagement**, on the other hand, tends to lead with its ears—listening to what parents think, dream, and worry about. The goal of **family engagement** is not to serve clients, but to gain partners. (Ferlazzo, 2011, pp. 10–14).

RESOURCES: INCLUSIVE PARTNERING AND CAPACITY BUILDING LEARNING STRATEGIES

Engaging families is an opportunity for continuous learning. As described in Chapter 2, family engagement refers to a range of activities that foster an integration and exchange of knowledge, information, and ideas and, all the while, a structured cosharing of decision making. Weyer's (2015) analysis of thirty-seven studies regarding family engagement research found that the benefits of families actively engaged (i.e., communicating their expectations with educators, co-creating goals, etc.) consistently outweigh families simply attending meetings at the school and participating in school activities. Henderson and Mapp's (2002) review of eighty parent involvement studies concluded that "when programs and initiatives focus on building respectful and trusting relationships among school staff, families, and community members, they are more effective in creating and sustaining connections that support student achievement" (p. 43). With the foundation, we highlight learning activities that can be used to foster communication, build inclusive cultural values, and provide opportunities for parent, family, and community voices.

High impact programs and learning strategies such as Academic Parent-Teacher Teams, Parent-Teacher Home Visits, Family Engagement Partnering Programs, and Community-Based Organizing Efforts are evidence based and known to produce difference-making results in family and community engagement and partnering fields. These programs center on student achievement (Epstein, 2011; Paredes, 2011) coaching and teaching key skills to parents and families about academic learning (Hoover-Dempsey & Sandler, 1997), and "an opportunity for teachers to improve their skills for effectively interacting with minority parents" (Paredes, 2011, p. 10). This final chapter offers brief summaries of some high impact programs as suggested resources to use when planning and completing your Action Plan (Chapter 8). The latter part of the chapter lists some lower impact, well-known technology-based, and practical learning strategies (EdSource, 2014b; Warren, Hong, Rubin, & Uy, 2009).

The planning tools you used in Chapter 8 will help restructure and enhance any of the learning activities as you plan, implement, and assess culturally proficient family and community engagement strategies. Table 9.1 is designed as a resource as you use the 7 Cs (Chapter 5) to guide your incorporation of The Essential Elements of Cultural Proficiency (Chapter 1). Consideration of the 7 Cs and the Essential Elements will guide you and your community partners as you co-create and revise your engagement and partnering strategies. Meaningful conversations about the 7 Cs and the Essential Elements are likely to ensure authentic, culturally proficient partnerships.

Academic Parent-Teacher Teams, Parent-Teacher Home Visit Projects, Family Engagement Partnering Programs, and Community-Based Organizing Efforts continue to gain traction as results demonstrate stronger and positive relationships, and improved student academic achievement (Faber, 2015; Mapp, 2003), particularly when an internal, systemic process is sustained. Reviewing these learning activities will be helpful to you as you continue on your journey to plan, commit, and take action.

ACADEMIC PARENT-TEACHER TEAMS (APTT)

Academic Parent-Teacher Teams provide an alternative approach to the regular parent-teacher conference meetings. Maria Paredes of WestEd describes APTT as "a research and evidence-based family engagement framework and best practice that aligns grade level learning skills, student performance data, and family-teacher communication and collaboration in order to inform and enrich the way families support learning at home" (2015, p. 6). The implementation of APTT means that teachers

TABLE 9.1

Essential Elements and the 7 Cs School and Interaction Inventory

Learning Strategy	Essential Element	7 Cs Strategies Used	Event Scheduled	Targeted Audience	Audience Trends
Resources	• Assessing Cultural Knowledge • Valuing Diversity • Managing the Dynamics of Difference • Adapting to Diversity • Institutionalizing Cultural Knowledge	• Collaboration • Communication • Caring • Culture • Connectedness • Community • Collective Responsibility	(e.g., Month, Day of Week, Time)	(e.g., Sixth Grade Families)	(e.g., Attendance for current and past few years)
(Career Day) as illustration	*Valuing Diversity* *Institutionalizing Cultural Knowledge*	*Communication* *(e.g., Flyers, School Calendar, Web page)*	*April 10*	*Third-fifth grade families*	*Increased by fifteen families*
(Fall Band Parent Meeting)					

Source: Adapted from Hooper, M., & Bernhardt, V. (2017). *Creating Capacity for Learning and Equity in Schools: Instructional, Adaptive, and Transformational Leadership*, p. 112.

 Available for download at **resources.corwin.com/CPPartnership**

become academic team leaders of entire classroom families, and families and teachers practice collaborative responsibility in setting goals. The strength in this approach is that they become equal partners in helping students improve their academic skills.

- **Parent-Teacher Home Visit Project** (http://www.pthvp.org). The Parent/Teacher Home Visit Project is a national nonprofit organization that encourages opportunities for educators to visit families to build and strengthen "relationships to support student learning" (Faber, 2015). It was co-created by parents, teachers, and community organizers to transform communities and build authentic partnering relationships. The central purpose is "to get to know each other and focus on the parent's hopes and dreams for his or her child" (p. 26–27). Home visits provide great insight to the funds of cultural knowledge families bring to schools and are key to breaking down implicit bias about students. In his article "Connecting With Students and Families Through Home Visits" (2015), Nick Faber, Board President of the National Parent-Teacher Home Visits Program, writes about incorporating home visits as a part of Saint Paul, Minnesota's inclusive partnering and capacity building strategy. When his district first began visiting parents, the funding was provided through a grant initiated by the local chapter of the American Federation of Teachers (AFT) in Saint Paul/Minneapolis. Educators, in pairs, enter the home without any materials for the first visit. They ask specific questions of the family to indicate that "we, as educators, see them as an asset" (p. 27). The findings of this program indicated that 76 percent of the teachers who participated changed their assumptions about parents, 93 percent reported that they learned something new about their students, and some teachers called it "their favorite part of the year, or their job" (p. 27). In essence, the evaluation of the home visit program reported that teachers and families' relationships strengthened to advocate for resources for children's needs (Faber, 2015). The AFT and the district are now looking at digital home visits to enhance this project.

- **Family Engagement Partnering Programs: Parent Universities and Parent Institutes.** Many schools, districts, and families have co-created structured programs that support sustained engagement. Incorporated into the success of these programs are these two suggestions:

  1. Offer curricula for families through technological methods such as online, hybrid learning, coaching guides, and face-to-face formats. Offering trainings or programs that can be viewed later by families affords the opportunity for them to view family and community events they may not have been able to attend.

  2. Co-present materials and trainings with community members or with family members. This method demonstrated the true partnerships in the development and presentation of goals, plans, and programs.

PARENT/FAMILY UNIVERSITIES

"School leaders are saying one of the best-known ways to involve parents is to establish a 'Parent University' program" (EdSource, 2014b). The idea of Parent Universities is not new, but the restructuring of them is appealing. Parent Universities vary from trainings and classes developed to teach parents how to help their children navigate through the school systems to offering regional information sessions and setting up a hotline for questions. Class sessions are usually taught with simultaneous translations for families in a language they understand, and offered in schools, district offices, and community centers. Curricula are designed and focused on family and community needs and feedback, so there's not a one-size-fits-all university program (Ferlazzo, 2011).

- **Parent Institute for Quality Education (PIQE)** (http://www.piqe.org/about/). An example of community-based organizing is The Parent Institute for Quality Education. This parent institute began in San Diego when community members Dr. Alberto Ochoa, a professor at San Diego State University, and Rev. Mardirosian became concerned about the low academic achievement of the students in their neighborhood. Initially, a meeting was scheduled with parents and families to discuss what might be some of the factors contributing to the situation. The one meeting was so impactful it evolved into eight weekly sessions. Now, this community organizing effort offers a nine-week session for families and schools. PIQE is designed to equip and empower parents with knowledge and skills about schools, the educational system, and how families can help their child and young adult be successful in the school (http://www.piqe.org/about/).

COMMUNITY-BASED ORGANIZING EFFORTS

Research about community organizing efforts reports results similar to the findings of increased parent and family engagement studies. Successful community organizing efforts are evidenced when community members work together with school personnel to enhance student success and address community issues (see the example in the Introduction). These community members can be faith-based members or organizations, clergy, businesses, nonprofit organizations, civic groups, or social and culturally based groups. The Harvard Graduate School of Education (Harvard Family Research Project, 2003) studied school-community collaborations "to engage parents in schools in low-income urban communities." The study, "Transforming Schools Through Community Organizing: A Research Review" proposed profitable connections for schools and students when parent and community-based cultural and social capital is valued. Community organizing data indicated that "efforts by community organizing helped to open new school facilities, the creation of small schools, implement health and safety programs, new academic programs in math and science, and increased professional development opportunities for teachers" (EdSource, 2014a, p. 10). "Policy implementations should not only include 'what's implementable and works', but also consider community values and needs and the interaction between policies, people, diverse communities, and teachers/staff and places" (Honig, 2006, p. 2). Listening to and collaborating with community members can bring social change, increase equitably focused policies, and meet the interests of the community at large (Warren, Hong, Rubin, & Uy, 2009).

RESOURCES: TECHNOLOGY SUPPORTED STRATEGIES

Technology supported strategies are frequently used for communication, but clearly, they are used in most of our applications of everyday learning. Establishing and creating school social media accounts such as Twitter, Facebook, and Instagram are pertinent to reaching out and communicating with parents in the twenty-first century. Numerous apps are available and geared to inform families of homework assignments, future school meeting date events, and their child's or youth's progress. It seems that more equitable and team-focused strategies are the most frequently used strategies to inform, invite, and recruit parents (Allen, 2007).

Announcements

Schools are used to making announcements both within the school and to the communities they serve. Announcements take many forms and can be issued at every opportunity. Sending flyers or printed notes home by students are still appropriate methods of communicating with parents and families. Print materials are still used, but schools have been successful when they go "straight to the source." Increasingly, communication with families is done more through *social media*, *text messaging*, and *electronic mail* than through flyers or print materials (Allen, 2007; Olender, Elias, & Mastroleo, 2010). Technology is well known for spreading information to large groups and is therefore a useful tool for contacting many people at one time. A "big" *marquee, email blasts, group texting*, or *Facebook postings* are fast and efficient ways to send messages to church/faith-based affiliations, civic and community organization members, and neighborhood businesses. *Google classrooms* and *Edmodo* are systems used to share assignments and announcements with students and parents. *Google translation* and other *translation tools* can help provide access to linguistically diverse parents and families (Andrade, 2015).

Information

Contacting parents to inform them of absences, school meetings, conferences, and classroom newsletters is sometimes done through *mass automated calls* or *phone blasts. Websites, homework hotlines, blogs, Wikipages,* and *teacher web pages* often offer information to keep families informed. When responding to a parent's question or request, acknowledge their request and respond in an appropriate time frame. In order to maintain respect with families and communities, if you say you're going to contact them or follow up with them, do so. It is a way of honoring them and honoring yourself. Responding demonstrates your high level of commitment and resolution to them (Hanover Research, 2014).

Sign-Up Sheets and Places to Volunteer

Providing opportunities for people to register interest in volunteering can be announced in many forms ranging from social media technology to the time-honored paper sign-up sheets. Online notifications can inform when and where there are opportunities to partner. The school's website, the *Family and Community Engagement FB page, or Wikipage* can also offer a place to make suggestions for improvement regarding a process, activity, or event (Weyer, 2015).

Surveys and Data. Data generated from surveys are useful tools that can be distributed and collected either online or in person. They are commonly used to give feedback and inform school leaders about the school climate. *Surveys* can be as brief as three questions/statements such as (1) tell us what you want to see in your child's learning; (2) what time of day, or day of the week is best for you to meet; (3) what type of family training would best help us help your child or youth? In 2015, the state of Utah enacted an online survey to collect information on parents' and families' perceptions of schools, and whether or not schools were successful in their engagement practices and policies (Weyer, 2015). Data is also shared with families through various reporting and *assessment applications* and programs. This is helpful for families to see grades, absences, missing assignments, and upcoming class projects (Hanover Research, 2014).

A warning, though . . . being conscientious about what we put in writing is vital as these technological messages are permanent and can be retrieved years later. On some occasions, insensitive communications make it to the forefront, so please check before sending your messages. When sending notes, flyers, emails, and other announcements, culturally proficient schools

1. Review the printed/written announcements for culturally insensitive language, graphics, or statements;

2. Represent the constituents of families and community members they serve;

3. Invite, recruit, involve, and include constituencies of family and community members as partners in decision-making, policy creating programs, and services who model advocacy for social justice;

4. Provide written announcements in languages that meet the needs of populations served;

5. Make information coherent; and

6. Emphasize the value of equity.

RESOURCES: PRACTICAL LEARNING STRATEGIES

The realities of today's busy lives impact family members' time and energy—the use of technology, working more than one job, financially running a single-family home, and driving long commutes impact family members' time and energy. With that in mind, we find that common sense coupled with some savviness increases levels of engagement. For instance, proactively contacting families regarding the student's positive behavior makes an indelible and good first impression. Too often families are contacted regarding their children's behavior only when something negative has happened, which perpetuates negative and strained relationships among families, schools, and communities. While engaged in speaking positively about the student, the teacher or administrator can extend an invitation to the family member to future school events or meetings where the family member's participation might well lead to a long-lasting, meaningful, and important experience and relationship. Henderson & Mapp's (2002) work emphasizes that when families know one person at a school, that makes a positive difference in the lives of children.

In this section are time-tested strategies to welcome and engage family members to schools. Using these strategies with a Cultural Proficiency lens offers respect and honor to family members and their children while providing opportunities to engage in their child's learning.

Undoubtedly, you are familiar with many of these learning strategies. As you review them, think of how the Essential Elements are embedded in the planning. Think of the Cs and which ones are applicable. How many of the Cs will be used or were used as a part of developing the event? Are you being intentional as you plan the learning?

As you continue to plan, take a look back in Chapter 8 at Figure 8.2. Where did you and/or your group place your school or district relative to Cultural Proficiency's Essential Elements? Based on your responses from Figure 8.2, how will you co-create strategies that will help in your school's growth or movement toward Cultural Proficiency? What kinds of strategies are conducive to your growth? As you consider the possibilities, review the following learning strategies. As you read, think about the potential changes you can make to ensure access, equity, and inclusion.

- **Assemblies** such as **award programs** provide the opportunity for a child or youth to be praised or acknowledged publicly for their achievements and accomplishments.

- **Beginning of school/welcome back activities**. Welcoming families at the very beginning of school is often stressful for teachers, counselors, and administrators, but it's exciting for families! Besides inviting families to *back-to-school night*, another strategy to use at the beginning of the school year involves compiling a list of students who are doing well behaviorally, academically, and socially.

- **Career Day.** An event where community members can present and describe their areas of expertise and share their skills. Guest speakers demonstrate their interest in the welfare of students becoming functioning and educated members of the community. Musicians, police officers, entrepreneurs, artists, counselors, and construction workers may be interested in serving in some capacity, wherever they can contribute.

- **Celebrating cultures**. There are many times throughout the school year that schools celebrate the contributions of various ethnic groups, women, and people with disabilities. These celebrations are also viewed as opportunities for learning about other people's cultures.

- **Child care.** Child care services offer families a chance to attend meetings and school functions while getting assistance with the responsibilities of parenthood or *familyhood*.

- **Classroom visits** provide family members the opportunity to observe children in their everyday school environment.

- **Combinations of activities.** Combining tasks to be more efficient with our time has become a natural phenomenon to us. Who would have thought thirty years ago that a telephone would also be used as a camera, a flashlight, and a way to send messages? Think of the many ways that several events and activities can be combined to save educators and families time.

- **Community liaison.** Create a position on your staff (full time or part time) to connect the school and the community with resources, businesses, and events.

- **Community Day (or the name of the city, area, county).** There may be persons such as historians, veterans, Holocaust survivors (or their children), military, business owners, fraternities, sororities, and people in various working positions who may have interests that could be coupled with what you need at the school.

- **Community/Parade Day.** What is your community known for? What are its historical events? As you become a frequent visitor to community businesses, you'll become increasingly familiar with businesspeople, service clubs, and community organizations.

- **Contact churches/faith-based institutions/community businesses.** Churches, community organizations, and civic and social groups in the community can provide important information and facilitate contact with families.

- **Flexibility.** Families appreciate it when teachers and administrators can allow for flexibility with schedules. This may be challenging to offer at times but hopefully there may be opportunities to build trust to provide a more open schedule, particularly for those families who are reaching out to you.

- **Food.** An effective common ground is when people come together to share food. When the school provides a light meal, the family member is freed from having to go home after work to prepare a meal and then go to the school meeting.

- **Free.** If you can afford to offer services or events at a discounted rate or for free, that's a great opportunity for families. If funding is a challenge, community businesses, including dental and medical health offices, often help sponsor teams and school organizations.

- **Grade level or school campus tours.** Schedule times for families and community members to tour your campus. Allow them time to visit classrooms or attend a workshop about the district.

- **Incentives.** A drawing or a prize is another way to motivate families' return of documents or communicating back with the school. Knowing that there's a possibility for their child to win something is worth signing that document or completing that survey!

- **Pair a passion.** To foster connectedness, some schools often pair a student, a class, a club, or a sport with someone at the school or in the community who shares that passion. For example, former athletes, band members, and others often offer their time to tutor or chaperone events or school trips.

- **Parent or Family Ambassadors** are family members who work with schools and families as group or parent leaders. They can be hired and trained to supervise children during recess or after-school tutoring, help in the classroom, or with Saturday school events.

- **Performances** are opportunities for children to demonstrate their talents and gifts at an event such as a festival, concert, play, or talent showcase. Many students have an array of unique talents that they can share with their classmates, their teachers, and community members. Student skills and accomplishments are also demonstrated through sports, drill team, speech and debate teams, spelling bees, art displays, and science projects.

- **Resource Centers** are designated spaces or rooms at school to provide materials for parents, families, and community members. Access to computers and reading materials in various languages can provide an atmosphere of collective learning and responsibility.

- **Shared space.** School facilities are used to host community members or organizations to help to bring the community to the school.

Now that you've had a chance to review the list of learning strategies, ask each member of your team to list all of the interactions and learning strategies they use with family and community members using the first column of Table 9.1. An example of a learning strategy (Career Day) is used in the first row. With which of the Essential Elements (Chapter 1) are you aligning your learning strategy? Put your response in the second column. The third column represents the 7 Cs from Chapter 5. Which of the 7 Cs are you incorporating into the learning strategy? Are all of them being used in several strategies or are you intentionally addressing one of them? Are there any missing or not being considered over a period of time? The fourth column requires event details to be completed. The fifth column focuses on the group(s) or audience for your event. The last column is open for you to note information regarding the recent trends of those events and strategies: How many people attended the last time the learning strategy was offered?

Compile individual lists to make a comprehensive list of the strategies your team uses. As you co-create with families and community members the implementation of the strategies you've chosen, use Table 9.1 as a guide to chart the impact of your actions as a whole group. Identify which events were attended by the greatest number of families. What strategies worked well? How will you revise some of the more *traditional* strategies to accommodate change? How will you provide for more inclusive accommodations and opportunities for these events? Ask for feedback on how to make them culturally proficient in every step of the developing process for the strategy.

SUMMARY

As the titles of the last two chapters indicate, commitment, planning, and actions are natural parts of any growth process. Committing to engage families means that you are committed to learning, growing, processing, and evaluating your own thoughts, behaviors, and actions.

Dr. Carol Dweck's research (2007) on achievement and success identified two core mindsets on how people approached challenges: fixed mindset and growth mindset. A fixed mindset person does not believe in effort and often gives up easily when faced with a challenge. People with a growth mindset continue to work toward change and see setbacks as useful. The mindset approach helps to examine your thoughts and beliefs in order to better understand how personal and/or institutional beliefs shape leadership styles, collaboration, and change. Through self-knowledge and perception, you can adjust your behavior to be in a *growth* pattern of learning. Remember that

- Demonstrating respect to families and community members begins before interactions

- Inviting family and community members as partners in the planning process communicates that their participation is valued prior to invitations sent or meetings held

- Working together to contribute to the welfare and well-being of children is a powerful reminder of the influence we have on each other

Your behaviors demonstrate your commitment to assessing your own culture, valuing diversity, and promoting equity and inclusion.

BE INTENTIONAL ABOUT IT

Your role as an educator greatly influences and impacts the students, families, and community of your school. As a teacher, commit to reflecting on your own attitudes and beliefs, creating curriculum and instruction, applying discipline equitably, and providing inclusive opportunities to partner with family members served by your school. As a leader, commit to reflecting on your leadership, vision, and collegiality in reaching out to family and community members. As a leader, commit and reflect upon the support you give to educator colleagues and community members as you build capacity and as they make their own commitments toward their journeys. As a school board member, commit to creating and approving policies that are equitable and inclusive of families and their communities in all their diversity. Commit to resources for the schools to move forward and achieve their goals of inclusion and access to equitable opportunities and outcomes.

We are enthused about your interest in and commitment to families, schools, and communities. We hope that you'll have fun partnering with families and building capacity in your school communities. We'd love to hear about your challenges, opportunities, and successes. Our commitment to you is to share our learning experiences and continuously learn from you, your challenges and successes.

It really doesn't matter where you are in the process; have fun planning, committing, and being intentional!

Resource A

BOOK STUDY GUIDE

Reflection and Dialogue are essential processes for individuals and organizations engaged in a journey toward Cultural Proficiency.

- Reflection is the discussion we have with ourselves to understand our values and behaviors.

- Dialogue is the discussion we have with others to understand their values and behaviors.

The following sets of questions are devised to support your learning. The questions are designed for your personal use as well as for professional use with colleagues.

CHAPTER 1—THE CULTURAL PROFICIENCY FRAMEWORK: TOOLS FOR FAMILY, SCHOOL, AND COMMUNITY ENGAGEMENT

Content Questions to Consider

- How might you describe the four Tools of Cultural Proficiency to someone who has not read the chapter?

- In what ways do you understand Overcoming the Barriers and the Guiding Principles to reflect core values, albeit one is negative, the other constructive?

- In what ways do the Essential Elements serve as standards for professional practice? And as guidelines in developing school and district policies and practices?

Personal Reaction Questions to Consider

- What is your reaction, personally and professionally, to the utility of the tools?

- What more do you want to know about the Cultural Proficiency Framework and its attendant tools?

- In what ways do you plan to use the rubric?

CHAPTER 2—THE *WHY* OF ENGAGEMENT

Content Questions to Consider

- In what ways might you describe the evolution of terminology such as from *family and community involvement* to *family and community engagement*?

- What is your understanding of Culturally Proficient Engagement?

Personal Reaction Questions to Consider

- In what ways do you describe your commitment to inclusive family and community engagement? What more would you like to do to demonstrate your commitment?

CHAPTER 3—THE MORAL IMPERATIVE FOR PARTNERSHIPS: HISTORICAL, LEGAL, AND EDUCATIONAL POLICY CONTEXTS

Content Questions to Consider

- How might you summarize a historical, legal, and educational context for family and community engagement when talking with a colleague?

- In what ways might you describe the evolution of family and community engagement since the initial 1965 authorization of the Elementary and Secondary Education Act?

Personal Reaction Questions to Consider

- In what ways does this chapter inform your understanding of cultural deficit approaches to students' educational opportunities?

- What questions are surfacing for you at this point of your reading this book?

CHAPTER 4—HOW CULTURAL PROFICIENCY INTERSECTS WITH FAMILY ENGAGEMENT

Content Questions to Consider

- When reading Table 4.1, what connections do you make among the work of Epstein, Constantino, Mapp, and Kuttner, and the Guiding Principles of Cultural Proficiency?

- In what ways do you understand reflection and dialogue as asset-based strategies for educators to use?

- How might the 9 Guiding Principles Key Questions inform your school or district's stated core values?

Personal Reaction Questions to Consider

- When you read the term *moral imperative*, what thoughts or reactions occur to you?

- In what ways did you react when reading and considering the 9 Guiding Principles Key Questions?

CHAPTER 5—THE 7 CS OF ENGAGEMENT

Content Questions to Consider

- What is your understanding of the intent of the 7 Cs?

- How might you summarize the 7 Cs?

Personal Reaction Questions to Consider

- How might family and community members see evidence of the 7 Cs in your school, district, and community? How might the members see evidence of the 7 Cs in your professional practice?

CHAPTER 6—BARRIERS TO FAMILY, SCHOOL, AND COMMUNITY ENGAGEMENT

Content Questions to Consider

- How might you describe barriers to cultural competence/proficiency to a colleague?

- How might you describe *systemic oppression*?

- How might you describe *privilege* and *entitlement*?

- In what ways does the Family and Community Engagement Rubric deepen your understanding of the Tools of Cultural Proficiency?

Personal Reaction Questions to Consider

- What is it about this chapter that will inform your work as an educator?

- What barriers to family and community engagement do you see in your school or district?

CHAPTER 7—THE GUIDING PRINCIPLES FOSTER ESSENTIAL ELEMENTS AS EDUCATOR AND SCHOOL ACTION

Content Questions to Consider

- In what ways do the Guiding Principles inform and support the Essential Elements?

- How might the Family and Community Engagement Rubric deepen your understanding of the Barriers as negative core values and the Guiding Principles as constructive core values?

Personal Reaction Questions to Consider

- In considering your role as an educator, in what ways do you describe overcoming barriers as a personal commitment?

- In what ways will you work with colleagues to ensure that your school or district adheres to core values that are inclusive of all cultural communities served by your school or district?

CHAPTER 8—THE 8TH C—COMMIT TO ACTION

Content Questions to Consider

- Returning to Table 8.1, how would you summarize the differences between the two columns?

- In what ways do you react to *planning to plan*? What meaning does it hold for you and your school or district?

Personal Reaction Questions to Consider

- In what ways might you advocate for planning to plan in your school or district? In what ways is equity central to this concept of *planning to plan*?

CHAPTER 9—RESOURCES: CULTURALLY PROFICIENT PLANNING FOR INCLUSIVE PARTNERING AND CAPACITY BUILDING

Content Questions to Consider

- What content in this chapter is most meaningful to you?

- In what ways might you use the tiers of resources presented in this chapter?

Personal Reaction Questions to Consider

- What more do you and your school or district need to do to be inclusive of all cultures to the benefit of all students?

Resource B

CULTURAL PROFICIENCY BOOKS' ESSENTIAL QUESTIONS

Corwin Cultural Proficiency Books	Authors	Focus and Essential Questions
Cultural Proficiency: A Manual for School Leaders, 4th ed., 2018	Randall B. Lindsey Kikanza Nuri-Robins Raymond D. Terrell	This book is an introduction to Cultural Proficiency. The book provides readers with extended discussion of each of the tools and the historical framework for diversity work. • What is Cultural Proficiency? How does Cultural Proficiency differ from other responses to diversity? • In what ways do I incorporate the Tools of Cultural Proficiency into my practice? • How do I use the resources and activities to support professional learning? • How do I identify barriers to student learning? • How do the guiding principles and essential elements support better education for students? • What does the *inside-out* process mean for me as an educator? • How do I foster challenging conversations with colleagues? • How do I extend my own learning?
Culturally Proficient Instruction: A Guide for People Who Teach, 3rd ed., 2012	Kikanza Nuri-Robins Randall B. Lindsey Delores B. Lindsey Raymond D. Terrell	This book focuses on the 5 Essential Elements and can be helpful to anyone in an instructional role. This book can be used as a workbook for a study group. • What does it mean to be a culturally proficient instructor? • How do I incorporate Cultural Proficiency into a school's learning community processes? • How do we move from *mindset* or *mental model* to a set of practices in our school?

(Continued)

Corwin Cultural Proficiency Books	Authors	Focus and Essential Questions
		• How does my *cultural story* support being effective as an educator with my students? • In what ways might we apply the Maple View Story to our learning community? • In what ways can I integrate the guiding principles of Cultural Proficiency with my own values about learning and learners? • In what ways do the Essential Elements as standards inform and support our work with the Common Core Standards? • How do I foster challenging conversations with colleagues? • How do I extend my own learning?
The Culturally Proficient School: An Implementation Guide for School Leaders, **2nd ed., 2013**	Randall B. Lindsey Laraine M. Roberts Franklin CampbellJones	This book guides the reader to examine their school as a cultural organization and to design and implement approaches to dialogue and inquiry. • In what ways do *Cultural Proficiency* and *school leadership* help me close achievement gaps? • What are the communication skills I need to master to support my colleagues when focusing on achievement gap topics? • How do *transactional* and *transformational* changes differ and inform closing achievement gaps in my school/district? • How do I foster challenging conversations with colleagues? • How do I extend my own learning?
Culturally Proficient Coaching: Supporting Educators to Create Equitable Schools, **2nd ed. 2020**	Delores B. Lindsey Richard S. Martinez Randall B. Lindsey	This book aligns the Essential Elements with Costa and Garmston's Cognitive Coaching model. The book provides coaches, teachers, and administrators a personal guidebook with protocols and maps for conducting conversations that shift thinking in support of all students achieving at levels higher than ever before. • What are the coaching skills I need in working with diverse student populations?

Corwin Cultural Proficiency Books	Authors	Focus and Essential Questions
		• In what ways do the Tools of Cultural Proficiency and Cognitive Coaching's States of Mind support my addressing achievement issues in my school? • How do I foster challenging conversations with colleagues? • How do I extend my own learning?
Culturally Proficient Inquiry: A Lens for Identifying and Examining Educational Gaps, 2008	Randall B. Lindsey Stephanie M. Graham R. Chris Westphal Jr. Cynthia L. Jew	This book uses protocols for gathering and analyzing student achievement and access data. Rubrics for gathering and analyzing data about educator practices are also presented. A CD accompanies the book for easy downloading and use of the data protocols. • How do we move from the *will* to educate all children to actually developing our *skills* and doing so? • In what ways do we use the various forms of student achievement data to inform educator practice? • In what ways do we use access data (e.g., suspensions, absences, enrollment in special education or gifted classes) to inform schoolwide practices? • How do we use the four rubrics to inform educator professional learning? • How do I foster challenging conversations with colleagues? • How do I extend my own learning?
Culturally Proficient Leadership: The Personal Journey Begins Within, 2nd ed., 2018	Raymond D. Terrell Eloise K. Terrell Delores B. Lindsey Randall B. Lindsey	This book guides the reader through the development of a cultural autobiography as a means to becoming an increasingly effective leader in our diverse society. The book is an effective tool for use by leadership teams. • How did I develop my attitudes about others' cultures? • When I engage in intentional cross-cultural communication, how can I use those experiences to heighten my effectiveness? • In what ways can I grow into being a culturally proficient leader?

(Continued)

Corwin Cultural Proficiency Books	Authors	Focus and Essential Questions
		• How do I foster challenging conversations with colleagues?
		• How do I extend my own learning?
Culturally Proficient Learning Communities: Confronting Inequity Through Collaborative Curiosity, 2009	Delores B. Lindsey Linda D. Jungwirth Jarvis V.N.C. Pahl Randall B. Lindsey	This book provides readers a lens through which to examine the purpose, the intentions, and the progress of learning communities to which they belong or wish to develop. School and district leaders are provided protocols, activities, and rubrics to engage in actions focused on the intersection of race, ethnicity, gender, social class, sexual orientation, and identity, faith, and ableness with the disparities in student achievement. • What is necessary for a learning community to become a *culturally proficient learning community*? • What is organizational culture and how do I describe my school's culture in support of equity and access? • What are *curiosity* and *collaborative curiosity*, and how do I foster them at my school/district? • How will *breakthrough questions* enhance my work as a learning community member and leader? • How do I foster challenging conversations with colleagues? • How do I extend my own learning?
The Cultural Proficiency Journey: Moving Beyond Ethical Barriers Toward Profound School Change, 2010	Franklin CampbellJones Brenda CampbellJones Randall B. Lindsey	This book explores Cultural Proficiency as an ethical construct. It makes transparent the connection between values, assumptions, and beliefs and observable behavior, making change possible and sustainable. The book is appropriate for book study teams. • In what ways does *moral consciousness* inform and support my role as an educator? • How do a school's *core values* become reflected in assumptions held about students? • What steps do I take to ensure that my school and I understand any low expectations we might have? • How do we recognize that our low expectations serve as ethical barriers?

Corwin Cultural Proficiency Books	Authors	Focus and Essential Questions
		• How do I foster challenging conversations with colleagues?
		• How do I extend my own learning?
Culturally Proficient Education: An Assets-Based Response to Conditions of Poverty, 2010	Randall B. Lindsey Michelle S. Karns Keith Myatt	This book is written for educators to learn how to identify and develop the strengths of students from low-income backgrounds. It is an effective learning community resource to promote reflection and dialogue. • What are *assets* that students bring to school? • How do we operate from an *assets-based* perspective? • What are my and my school's expectations about students from low-income and impoverished backgrounds? • How do I foster challenging conversations with colleagues? • How do I extend my own learning?
Culturally Proficient Collaboration: Use and Misuse of School Counselors, 2011	Diana L. Stephens Randall B. Lindsey	This book uses the lens of Cultural Proficiency to frame the American Association of School Counselors' performance standards and the Education Trust's Transforming School Counseling Initiative as means for addressing issues of access and equity in schools in collaborative school leadership teams. • How do counselors fit into achievement-related conversations with administrators and teachers? • What is the *new role* for counselors? • How does this *new role* differ from existing views of school counselors? • What is the role of site administrators in this new role of school counselor? • How do I foster challenging conversations with colleagues? • How do I extend my own learning?
A Culturally Proficient Society Begins in School: Leadership for Equity, 2011	Carmella S. Franco Maria G. Ott Darline P. Robles	This book frames the life stories of three superintendents through the lens of Cultural Proficiency. The reader is provided the opportunity to design or modify his or her own leadership for equity plan.

(Continued)

Corwin Cultural Proficiency Books	Authors	Focus and Essential Questions
		• In what ways is the role of school superintendent related to equity issues?
		• Why is this topic important to me as a superintendent or aspiring superintendent?
		• What are the leadership characteristics of a Culturally Proficient school superintendent?
		• How do I foster challenging conversations with colleagues?
		• How do I extend my own learning?
The Best of Corwin: Equity, 2012	Randall B. Lindsey, Ed.	This edited book provides a range of perspectives of published chapters from prominent authors on topics of equity, access, and diversity. It is designed for use by school study groups. • In what ways do these readings support our professional learning? • How might I use these readings to engage others in learning conversations to support all students learning and all educators educating all students?
Culturally Proficient Practice: Supporting Educators of English Learning Students, 2012	Reyes L. Quezada Delores B. Lindsey Randall B. Lindsey	This book guides readers to apply the 5 Essential Elements of Cultural Competence to their individual practice and their school's approaches to equity. The book works well for school study groups. • In what ways do I foster support for the education of English learning students? • How can I use action research strategies to inform my practice with English learning students? • In what ways might this book support all educators in our district/school? • How do I foster challenging conversations with colleagues? • How do I extend my own learning?
A Culturally Proficient Response to LGBT Communities: A Guide for Educators, 2013	Randall B. Lindsey Richard Diaz Kikanza Nuri-Robins Raymond D. Terrell Delores B. Lindsey	This book guides the reader to understand sexual orientation in a way that provides for the educational needs of all students. The reader explores values, behaviors, policies, and practices that impact lesbian, gay, bisexual, and transgender (LGBT) students, educators, and parents/guardians.

Corwin Cultural Proficiency Books	Authors	Focus and Essential Questions
		• How do I foster support for LGBT colleagues, students, and parents/guardians?
		• In what ways does our school represent a value for LGBT members?
		• How can I create a safe environment for all students to learn?
		• To what extent is my school an environment where it is safe for the adults to be open about their sexual orientation?
		• How do I reconcile my attitudes toward religion and sexuality with my responsibilities as a PreK–12 educator?
		• How do I foster challenging conversations with colleagues?
		• How do I extend my own learning?
Fish Out of Water: Mentoring, Managing, and Self-Monitoring People Who Don't Fit In, 2016	Kikanza Nuri-Robins Lewis Bundy	This book helps the reader manage the dynamics of difference by focusing on sustaining a healthy organizational culture using the Cultural Proficiency Continuum as a template. Strategies based on the Guiding Principles and the Essential Elements are provided for supporting both children and adults who are struggling to understand or use the cultural norms of a particular environment. A Study Guide is provided in the Resources so that the book can easily be used for professional development or a small group book study. • How do I determine the nature of diversity in this environment? • How might I understand who is thriving in this setting and who is not? • Are there any groups that are being targeted? • Are the rules of the environment oppressive to any individuals or groups in the environment? • Why are certain groups making the organizational rules for everyone? • How might I address systems to make the environment healthier? • What strategies are available to my colleagues and me as we seek to sustain a healthy, inclusive environment for all?

(Continued)

(Continued)

Corwin Cultural Proficiency Books	Authors	Focus and Essential Questions
		<ul><li>What strategies are available to an individual who is trying to succeed in a toxic environment?</li><li>How do I extend my own learning?</li></ul>
Guiding Teams to Excellence With Equity: Culturally Proficient Facilitation, 2017	John Krownapple	This book provides mental models and information for educators to develop as facilitators of professional learning and organizational change for equity in education. It also supports experienced professional development professionals with tools for doing their work in a culturally competent and proficient manner. This book is for organizations working to build internal capacity and sustainability for Cultural Proficiency.<ul><li>Assuming we value excellence and equity in education, why do we need Cultural Proficiency and culturally proficient facilitators of the process?</li><li>How can we use Cultural Proficiency as content (framework) and process (journey) to achieve excellence with equity?</li><li>What do facilitators do in order to work with teams in a culturally proficient manner?</li></ul>
Culturally Proficient Response to the Common Core: Ensuring Equity Through Professional Learning, 2015	Delores B. Lindsey Karen M. Kearney Delia Estrada Raymond D. Terrell Randall B. Lindsey	This book guides the reader to view and use the Common Core State Standards as a vehicle for ensuring all demographic groups of students are fully prepared for college and careers.<ul><li>In what ways do I use this book to deepen my learning about equity?</li><li>In what ways do I use this book to deepen my learning about CCSS?</li><li>In what ways do I use this book with colleagues to deepen our work on equity and on the CCSS?</li><li>How can I and we use the Action Planning guide as an overlay for our current school planning?</li></ul>

Corwin Cultural Proficiency Books	Authors	Focus and Essential Questions
Culturally Proficient Inclusive Schools: When All Means All, 2017	Delores B. Lindsey Jacqueline S. Thousand Cindy L. Jew Lori R. Piowlski	This book provides responses and applications of the 4 Tools of Cultural Proficiency for educators who desire to create and support classrooms and schools that are inclusive and designed intentionally to educate all learners. General educators and Special Educators will benefit from using the 5 Essential Elements and the tenets of Inclusive Schooling to create and sustain educational environments so that when we say *all* students, we truly mean *all* students will achieve at levels higher than ever before. • What might be some ways general and special educators can work collaboratively to create conditions for all students to be successful? • In what ways does this book address issues of equity and access for all students? • How do the 4 Tools of Cultural Proficiency inform the work of Inclusive Schooling? What's here for you? • In what ways does the Action Plan template offer opportunities for you and your colleagues? • For what are you waiting to help narrow and close equity gaps in your classroom and schools? • How do I foster challenging conversations about inclusive education with colleagues? • How do I extend my own learning about ways in which to facilitate inclusive learning environments?
The Cultural Proficiency Manifesto: Finding Clarity Amidst the Noise, 2017	Randal B. Lindsey	This book is a call to action for educators to ensure we are creating culturally inclusive and responsive environments for our students. • What are the Lessons Learned, the answers to which equip educators to address issues of inequity?

(Continued)

RESOURCE B   133

(Continued)

Corwin Cultural Proficiency Books	Authors	Focus and Essential Questions
		• In what ways do educators use the Tools of Cultural Proficiency in listening for clarity while living amidst turmoil? • What are behaviors of commitment in moving from practices of inequity to practices of equity?
Equity Partnerships: A Culturally Proficient Approach to Family, School, and Community Engagement	Angela R. Clark-Louque Randall B. Lindsey Reyes L. Quezada Cynthia L. Jew	This book provides guidance to educators intent on making culturally inclusive family and community engagement central to their professional practice as well as to the policies and practices. • What are the historical, social, and educational foundations for community engagement being a moral imperative for today's schools? • In what ways does the Cultural Proficiency Framework build on and inform the work of Epstein, Constantino, and Mapp and Kuttner? • How do we develop, initiate, monitor, and assess community engagement action plans? • How might I engage others to create a capacity building culture for partnering? • How might we intentionally execute an inclusive and equitable plan for family, school, and community engagement?

Resource C

AUTHORS, ORGANIZATIONS, AND WEBSITES

AUTHORS

Dr. Susan Auerbach

Professor, Educational Leadership and Policy Studies, California State University, Northridge

Research focus—parent/family engagement in schools, school-community partnerships, social context of urban education

Book: *School Leadership for Authentic Family and Community Partnerships: Research Perspectives for Transforming Practice* (2012).

Dr. James Comer

Comer School Development Program

Research focus—studies the social and developmental factors related to the impact nurturing families have on children's development, particularly families affected by poverty.

Book: *What I Learned in School: Reflections on Race, Child Development, and School Reform* (2009).

Dr. Anne Henderson

Senior Consultant, Community Involvement Program

Research focus—how to form partnerships with families and how to make them work.

Book: *Beyond the Bake Sale: The Essential Guide to Family School Partnerships* (2007).

Dr. Nancy Hill

Developmental Psychologist

Research focus—studies ways in which race, ethnicity, and socioeconomic status affect parents' beliefs and behaviors, which in turn affect children's mental health and behavior.

Book: *Ethnic Minority Youth and Parents Still Navigate Inequities in Educational Opportunities: New Tools for Old Problems* (2017).

Dr. William Jeynes

Professor of Education, California State University, Long Beach

Research focus—evaluates the effectiveness of parent involvement programs and identifies that involved teacher-parent partnerships, teacher-parent communication, checking homework, and shared reading are critical components.

Book: *Parental Involvement and Academic Success* (2010).

Dr. Karen Mapp

Harvard Graduate School of Education

US Department of Education

Research focus—researches the impact that family engagement has on literacy, attendance, and dropout rates.

Book: *Powerful Partnerships: A Teacher's Guide to Engaging Families for Student Success* (2017).

Dr. Debbie Pushor

Professor, University of Saskatchewan, Canada

Research focus—researches parent engagement in schooling and education.

Book: *Living as Mapmakers: Charting a Course With Children Guided by Parent Knowledge* (2015).

Dr. Reyes L. Quezada

Professor and Department Chair, Department of Learning and Teaching, School of Leadership and Education Sciences, University of San Diego

Research focus—family, school, and community engagement and partnerships

Book: *Family, School, Community Engagement and Partnerships: An Imperative for K-12, and Colleges of Education in the Development of 21st Century Educators* (2015).

Dr. Gail Thompson

Founder and CEO, Inspirations by Gail

Research focus—presents her work on school reform, parent involvement, and the schooling experiences of African American and Latinx students.

Book: *What African American Parents Want Educators to Know* (2003).

¡Bien Educados!

¡Bien Educados! is a project that partners with the Mid-Atlantic Equity Consortium (MAEC) and the Maryland Department of Education to provide information to schools, educators, and community (e.g., governmental, faith-based, and nonprofit) organizations. Their mission is to work with groups and organizations who are already serving Latinx families, and to provide information so Latinx families can better advocate for their children.

California Association for Bilingual Education Project 2-Inspire

http://www.gocabe.org/index.php/parents/project-2-inspire/

Project 2-Inspire Family Engagement Leadership Development Program is a research-based collaborative project that works with school districts to build capacity in establishing family-school-community leadership programs that involves all stakeholders. The program provides educators, parents, and community members with the skills needed to partner so they may support each other in the education of their children.

Family Engagement Framework

https://www.cde.ca.gov

To support strong, healthy, and systematic school, family, and community partnerships statewide, the California Department of Education (CDE) in connection with West Ed. developed a tool describing expectations and implementation strategies for integrated family engagement within state educational programs. The Family Engagement Framework is intended to provide guidance to educators, districts, schools, families, and communities as they plan, implement, and evaluate strategies across multiple programs for effective family engagement to support student achievement and close the academic achievement gap.

Chicago Parent Center

To help reduce the dropout rate, Chicago's Parent Center model positively impacted the rate of graduation by 16 percent for each year that a parent was involved in the program. Their results found that parent participation effected children's academic success and social development.

Community Planning Toolkit

https://www.communityplanningtoolkit.org/community-engagement

This toolkit is designed to provide guidance on the issues to consider when planning and designing community engagement projects. It focuses on quality and effectiveness, process planning, and designing engagement tailored to the particular issue. Additional levels of participation, timeframe, and range of stakeholders are issues that are discussed in this toolkit.

Conexion Americas

http://www.conexionamericas.org/what-we-do/programs-and-services-for-latino-families/parents-as-partners/

This program delivers a six- to nine-week series of workshops designed to forge a working relationship between Latinx parents and schools. The purpose is to ultimately improve children's academic achievement. The program is delivered in Spanish and uses a specific curriculum for Pre-K, elementary, and middle school.

The sessions, which end with a parental graduation ceremony, teach parents to understand and navigate the school system through a series of workshops in Spanish, led by a team of trained parent facilitators. Strategies such as parent-to-parent approach aligned with the core value of building the skills of our participants and assisting them in being the principal agents of community change are hallmarks of excellence in this program.

Edutopia

https://www.edutopia.org/article/community-business-partnerships-resources

Edutopia supports schools on how schools can learn and benefit from the support and expertise of local businesses, organizations, and individuals, and discover strategies for fostering successful business and community partnerships.

Global Family Research Project

https://globalfrp.org/

The Global Family Research Project succeeded the Harvard Family Research Project (1983–2016). It separated from the Harvard Graduate School of Education on January. 1, 2017. It has an established track record in defining and advancing the fields of family, school, and community engagement through research utilizing case methodology to engage families in an ecology of learning.

Families and Schools Together (FAST)

Familiesandschools.org

FAST is a nonprofit organization that offers a program utilizing evidence-based practices. It offers four-phase programs for parents to help build social capital in schools and communities, and offers programs to schools to build supportive relationships with families.

Flamboyan Foundation

http://flamboyanfoundation.org/

This program brings together families and educators to support children in the educational arena. Educators have the opportunity to help families understand how to best support their student's learning at home. Students are surrounded by the support they need to excel socially, emotionally, and academically for the long term. Students do better when families and educators work together as equal partners.

This program targets families who are most impacted by inequality and works to strengthen family engagement in schools through our school partnerships and leadership development programs.

Institute of Education Sciences— US Department of Education

https://ies.ed.gov

The Institute of Education Sciences collects and analyzes data about all aspects of US schools and education, including English learners and students with disabilities.

National Center for Education Evaluation and Regional Assistance

https://ies.ed.gov/ncee/edlabs/regions/pacific/pdf/REL_2016148.pdf

The Toolkit of Resources for Engaging Families and the Community as Partners in Education is a four-part resource that brings together research, promising practices, and useful tools and resources to guide educators in strengthening partnerships with families and community members to support student learning. Based on defining family and community engagement as an overarching approach to support family well-being, strong parent–child relationships, and students' ongoing learning and development, the toolkit is designed to guide educators into building awareness of how their beliefs and assumptions about family and community engagement influence their interactions with families and the community and how knowledge about the demographic characteristics of the families in their schools can inform educators about what might support or hinder family engagement with schools.

Los Angeles Unified School District–Parents as Equal Partners

http://home.lausd.net/ourpages/pcsb/pubs/school_goals_engl.pdf

The Parents as Equal Partners in the Education of their Children Resolution, adopted by the Board of Education in December 2010, led to a series of recommendations for implementation at school sites. These recommendations include goals aligned to the mandates of No Child Left Behind (2001), the Parent as Equal Partners Task Force Recommendations (2011), and the California Department of Education Family Engagement Framework (2011). These goals and indicators provide guidance to schools in developing and implementing effective parental involvement policies and practices that yield higher levels of student academic success.

National Association for Family, School, and Community Engagement

https://nafsce.org

Professionals work together to support the mission of advancing policies and practices for families, schools, and communities.

National Black Parents Association

https://blackchildren.org

This organization seeks to empower Black parents to help foster the well-being of Black children. The purpose is to support and advocate improving the lives and education of Black children and families.

National Center for Family and Community Connections with Schools

https://www.sedl.org/connections/

The Center's purpose is to connect research, data, and resources about families and communities with student achievement in mathematics and reading.

Southwest Educational Development Laboratory or American Institutes for Research

www.sedl.org or air.org

The American Institutes for Research seek to connect research, policy, and practice in order to serve diverse populations. The goal is to use research to create strategies, ideas, and approaches for effective use in schools and family lives.

The National Center on Safe Supportive Learning Environments

https://safesupportivelearning.ed.gov/

The National Center on Safe Supportive Learning Environments offers information and technical assistance to states, districts, schools, institutions of higher learning, and communities focused on improving student supports and academic enrichment. We believe that with the right resources and support, educational stakeholders can collaborate to (1) provide all students with access to a well-rounded education, (2) improve school conditions for student learning, and (3) improve the use of technology so all students have the opportunity to realize academic success and digital literacy in safe and supportive learning environments.

The National Center on School, Family, and Community Partnerships

https://nnps.jhucsos.com/

The National Center on School, Family, and Community Partnerships conducts research on the nature and effects of family and community involvement, and through the National Network of Partnership Schools (NNPS) at Johns Hopkins University guides schools, districts, and states to implement research-based partnership programs.

The National Education Association

http://www.nea.org/home/49395.htm

The National Education Association provides resources for schools, teachers, and community organizations with tools on how to effectively engage families and partner with schools in the education of children.

The National Parent Teacher Association

https://www.pta.org/

Comprise millions of families, students, teachers, administrators, and business community leaders devoted to the educational success of students and their families.

PACER Center

www.pacer.org

PACER Center enhances the quality of life and expands opportunities for children, youth, and young adults with all disabilities and their families so each person can reach his or her highest potential. PACER operates on the principles of parents helping parents, supporting families, promoting a safe environment for all children, and working in collaboration with others. The program offers assistance to individual families, workshops, materials for parents and professionals, and leadership in securing a free and appropriate public education for all children.

The School Community Journal

http://www.schoolcommunitynetwork.org/SCJ.aspx

The School Community Journal is a refereed journal that includes research and field reports related to the school as a community of teachers, students, parents, and staff. The journal has been published twice annually since 1991—Spring/Summer and Fall/Winter.

The School Community Network

http://www.schoolcommunitynetwork.org/docs/FET_Booklet.pdf

The School Community Network (SCN) provides resources, trainings, and tools to build strong communities focused on student learning. SCN is sponsored by the Academic Development Institute (ADI), a not-for-profit organization located in Lincoln, Illinois. SCN's work draws from ADI's thirty-year experience and extensive research in family and community engagement.

United States Department of Education

https://www.ed.gov/parent-and-family-engagement

The United States Department of Education resources on family engagement focus on the belief that raising the next generation is a shared responsibility. When families, communities, and schools work together, students are more successful and the entire community benefits. For schools and districts across the United States, family engagement is becoming an integral part of education reform efforts.

References

Allen, JoBeth. (2007). *Creating welcoming schools: A practical guide to home-school partnerships with diverse families.* New York, NY: Teachers College Press.

Alvarez v. Board of Trustees of the Lemon Grove School District. (1931).

American Psychological Association. (2018). *School connectedness.* https://www.apa.org/pi/lgbt/programs/safe-supportive/school-connectedness/default.aspx

Andrade, David. (2015). The importance of communication in education. *Techlearning.* https://www.techlearning.com/tl-advisor-blog/8716

Assembly Bill 97. Cal. Stat. §§ 47-1-117 (2013). Local Control Funding Formula.

Associated Press. (2000, January 17). King's widow urges acts of compassion. *Los Angeles Times.*

Berkowitz, Ruth, Astor, Ron Avi, Pineda, Diana, DePedro, Kris Tunac, Weiss, Eugenia, & Benbenishty, Rami. (2017). Parental involvement and perceptions of school climate in California. *Urban Education,* 1–31. https://www.researchgate.net/publication/312658970_Parental_Involvement_and_Perceptions_of_School_Climate_in_California

Boonk, Lisa, Gijselaers, Heironymus, J. M., Ritzen, Henk, & Brand-Gruwel, Saskia. (2018). A review of the relationship between parental involvement indicators and academic achievement. *Educational Research Review, 24,* 10–30.

Bourdieu, Pierre. (1986). The forms of capital. In J. G. Richardson (Ed.), *Handbook of theory and research for the sociology of education* (pp. 241–258). New York, NY: Greenwood Press.

Branch, Taylor. (1998). *Pillar of fire: America in the King years, 1963–1965.* New York, NY: Simon & Schuster.

Bromberg, Marni, & Theokas, Christina. (2013). *Breaking the glass ceiling of achievement for low-income students and students of color.* Washington, DC: The Education Trust.

Brown v. Board of Education of Topeka, 347 U.S. 483 (1954).

Buttner, E. Holly. (2004). How do we "dis" students? A model of (dis)respectful business instructor behavior. *Journal of Management Education, 28*(3), 647–673.

California Department of Education. (2014). *Family engagement framework: A tool for California school districts.* California Department of Education in conjunction with WestEd. Sacramento, CA. https://www.cde.ca.gov/ls/pf/pf/documents/famengageframeenglish.pdf

Center for Culturally Proficient Educational Practice. (2018). https://ccpep.org

Center for Disease Control and Prevention. (2009, July). *Fostering school connectedness: Improving student health and academic achievement.* https://www.cdc.gov/healthyyouth/protective/pdf/connectedness_administrators.pdf

Chenoweth, Karin. (2017). *Schools that succeed: How educators marshal the power of systems for improvement.* Cambridge, MA: Harvard Education Press.

Clark, Glennie Bridgeforth. (1960). *Lessons of Life.* Sermon.

Clark-Louque, Angela R., Greer, Wilbert, Clay, April, & Balogun, Ayanna. (2017). "Doing well in spite of school": How African American students perceive achievement, engagement, and climate in the aftermath of California's Local Control Funding Formula. *Wisdom in Education Journal, 7*(2).

Clark-Louque, Angela R., & Latunde, Yvette. (2019). Addressing inequities in African American student achievement: Using cultural proficiency and a dual capacity building framework. *Frontiers in Education, 4,* https://doi.org/10.3389/feduc.2019.00033

Coleman, James S., & US National Center for Education Statistics. (1966). *Equality of educational opportunity* [Summary report]. Washington, DC: US Dept. of Health, Education, and Welfare, Office of Education.

Collins, James, & Porras, Jerry. (1997). *Built to last: Successful habits of visionary companies.* New York, NY: Harper.

Commission on Teacher Credentialing. (2014). *California professional standards for education leaders.* Sacramento, CA: Author.

Constantino, Steve. (2003). *Engaging all families: Creating a positive school culture by putting research into practice.* Lanham, MD: Rowan & Littlefield.

Cross, Terry L., Bazron, Barbara J., Dennis, Karl, & Isaacs, Mareasa R. (1989, March). *Toward a culturally competent system of care: A monograph on effective services for minority children who are severely emotionally disturbed.* Washington, DC: Georgetown, University Child Development Program, Child, and Adolescent Service System Program (CASSP Technical Assistance Center).

Dantas, L. Maria, & Manyak, C. Patrick. (2010). *Home-school connections in a multicultural society: Learning from and with culturally and linguistically diverse families.* New York, NY: Routledge.

DeNisco, Alison. (2018). *Report: Parents value engagement, but say schools fall short.* Collaborative for Customer-Based Execution and Strategy Benchmark K–12 School Study, 2017. Rice University. https://www.districtadministration.com/article/report-parents-value-engagement-say-schools-fall-short

Dettmer, Peggy, Knackendoffel, Ann, & Thurston, Linda P. (2012). *Collaboration, consultation and teamwork for students with special needs* (7th ed.). Upper Saddle River, NJ: Pearson.

Dettmer, Peggy, Thurston, Linda P., Knackendoffel, Ann, & Dyck, Norma. (2009). *Collaboration, consultation, and teamwork for students with special needs.* Upper Saddle River, NJ: Pearson.

DeWitt, Peter. (2018). *Do educators really want parents to be accountable?* http://blogs.edweek.org/edweek/finding_common_ground/2018/03/do_educators_really_want_parents_to_be_held_accountable.html

Dweck, Carol. (2007). *Mindset: The new psychology of success.* New York, NY: Ballantine Books.

EdSource. (2014a). *The power of parents: Research underscores the impact of parent involvement in schools.* https://edsource.org/wp-content/publications/Power-of-Parents-Feb-2014.pdf

EdSource. (2014b). *Parent Universities help districts tap into feedback required under funding formula.* https://edsource.org/2014/parent-universities-help-districts-tap-into-feedback-required-under-funding-formula/56778

Elementary and Secondary Education Act of 1965: H. R. 2362, 89th Cong., 1st sess., Pub. L. No. 89-10.

Epstein, Joyce L. (1991). Effects on student achievement in teachers' practice of parent involvement. *Advances in Reading/Language Research*, 5.

Epstein, Joyce L. (2011). *School, family, and community partnerships: Preparing educators and improving schools* (2nd ed.). Boulder, CO: Westview Press.

Epstein, Joyce L. (2015). Forward. In R. L. Quezada, V. Alexandrowicz, & S. Molina (Eds.), *Family, school, community engagement and partnerships: An imperative for K–12, and colleges of education in the development of 21st century educators.* UK. Routledge.

Epstein, Joyce L., Coates, Lucretia, Salinas, Karen Clark, Sanders, Mavis G., & Simon, Beth. (1997). *School, family, and community partnerships: Your handbook for action.* Thousand Oaks, CA: Corwin.

Epstein, Joyce L., & Dauber, Susan L. (1991). School programs and teacher practices of parent involvement in inner-city elementary and middle schools. *The Elementary School Journal*, *91*(3), 289–305.

Epstein, Joyce L., Sanders, Mavis G., Simon, Beth S., Salinas, Karen Clark, Jansorn, Natalie Rodriguez, & Van Voorhis, Frances L. (2002). *School, family, and community partnerships: Your handbook for action* (2nd ed.). Thousand Oaks, CA: Corwin.

Every Student Succeeds Act (2015). Pub. L. No. 114-95 § 114 Stat.1177 (2015–2016).

Faber, Nick. (2015). Connecting with students and families through home visits. https://www.aft.org/sites/default/files/ae_fall2015faber.pdf

Ferguson, C., Jordan, C., Wood, L., Rodriguez, V., & Buttram, J. (2005). Beyond the building: A facilitation guide for school family and community connections, p. 27. Austin, TX: Southwest Educational Development Laboratory.

Ferlazzo, Larry L. (2011). Involvement or engagement? Schools, families, communities. *School Leadership*, *68*(8), 10–14.

Ferlazzo, Larry, & Hammond, Lorie. (2009). *Building parent engagement in schools* (pp. 10–14). Sacramento, CA: Linworth Books.

Flamboyan Foundation. (2011). *Dos and don'ts: Communication with families around academics.* http://flamboyanfoundation.org/wp/wp-content/uploads/2011/07/Dos-and-Donts-Communication-with-Families-Around-Academics1.pdf

Flores, Peter, III, & Domingues, Joseph. (2017, January/February). Leading from the strawberry fields: Transformative leadership in Santa Maria. *Leadership*, Association of California School Administrators.

Foster, Marquita, Young, Jamaal R., & Young, Jemimah L. (2017). Teacher perceptions of parental involvement and the achievement of diverse learners: A meta-analysis. *Journal of Ethical Educational Leadership*, *4*(5), 1–17.

Friend, Lynn, & Cook, Marilyn. (1992). *Interactions: Collaboration skills for school professionals.* White Plains, NY: Longman.

Fullan, Michael. (2003). *The moral imperative of school leadership.* Thousand Oaks, CA: Corwin.

Gettinger, Maribeth, & Guetschow, Kristen Waters. (1998). Parental involvement in schools: Parent and teacher perceptions of roles, efficacy, and opportunities. *Journal of Research & Development in Education*, *32*(1), 38–52.

Global Family Research Foundation. (2018). *Joining together to create a bold vision for next generation family engagement: Engaging families to transform education.* New York, NY: Carnegie Corporation of New York.

González, Norma, Moll, Luis, & Amanti, Cathy. (2005). Funds of knowledge for teaching: Using a qualitative approach to connect homes and classrooms. In *Funds of knowledge: Theorizing practices in households, communities, and classrooms* (pp. 71–87). New Jersey: Lawrence Erlbaum Publishers.

Green, Judith A. (2008, November/December). Collaborating with special education administrators. *Principal*, 12–15.

Gruenert, Steve, & Whitaker, Todd. (2015). *School culture rewired: How to define, assess, and transform it.* Alexandria, VA: Association of Curriculum and Supervision Development.

Hanover Research. (2014). *Best practices in family and community engagement.* Author: www.hanoverresearch.com

Harvard Family Research Project. (2003). *Transforming schools through community organizing: A research review.* Family Involvement Network of Educators (FINE). Harvard Graduate School of Education.

Harvard Family Research Project. (2012). *Family engagement and children with disabilities: A resource guide for educators and parents.* https://www.brandeis.edu/lemberg/pdf/resources/FE-ChildrenWithDisabilities.pdf

Hawkins, B. Denise. (2016). *Diverse student populations are in the classroom: Are you prepared to meet their needs?* National Education Association. http://www.nea.org/home/66241.htm

Hawley, Willis. (1983). *Strategies for effective desegregation: Lessons from research.* Lexington, MA: Lexington Books.

Henderson, Anne T. (2016). *Quick brief on family engagement in Every Student Success Act.* Annenberg Institute for School Reform. Retrieved from https://ra.nea.org/wp-content/uploads/2016/06/FCE-in-ESSA-in-Brief.pdf

Henderson, Anne, Johnson, Vivian, Mapp, Karen, & Davies, Don. (2007). *Beyond the bake sale: The essential guide to family/school partnerships.* New York, NY: New Press.

Henderson, Anne T., & Mapp, Karen L. (2002). *A new wave of evidence: The impact of school, family, and community connections on student achievement.* Austin, TX: Southwest Educational Development Laboratory.

Henderson, Kaya. (2018, November 15). *We don't need saviors, we need leaders who are ready to form true partnerships with families and communities* [Blog post]. https://educationpost.org/network/kaya-henderson/

Hiatt-Michael, Diana. (1994, Fall/Winter). Parent involvement in American public schools: An historical perspective, 1642–2000. *School Community Journal*, 4(2).

Hirsch, Stephanie. (2010). Collective responsibility makes all teachers the best. *Teachers Teaching Teachers*, 6(1). https://learningforward.org/docs/leading-teacher/sept10_hirsh.pdf?sfvrsn=2

Honig, Meredith. (2006). *Complexity and policy implementation: Challenges and opportunities for the field.* New York: State University of New York Press.

Hooper, Mary, & Bernhardt, Victoria. (2017). *Creating capacity for learning and equity in schools: Instructional, adaptive, and transformational leadership.* New York: Routledge.

Hoover-Dempsey, Kathleen V. (1987). Parent involvement: Contributions of teacher efficacy, school socioeconomic status and other school characteristics. *American Educational Research Journal*, 24, 417–435.

Hoover-Dempsey, Kathleen V. & Sandler, Howard M. (1997). Why do parents become involved in their children's education? *Review of Educational Research, 67*(1), 3–42. https://doi.org/10.3102/00346543067001003

Individuals with Disabilities Education Act, 20 U.S. Code, § 1400 (2004).

International Classification of Functioning. (2001). *Pathways out of poverty for working families: A case study of the parent to parent, building to building, school to school project.* Battle Creek, MI: W. K. Kellogg Foundation.

Jorgenson, Derek, Farrell, Laura, Fudge, Julie L., & Pritchard, Andrew. (2018). *Journal of the Scholarship of Teaching and Learning, 18*(1), 75–95. https://files.eric.ed.gov/fulltext/EJ1169938.pdf

Kading, Marshall. (2015). *School connectedness: An analysis of students' relationship to school.* Winona State University. https://www.winona.edu/counseloreducation/media/school%20connectedness.pdf

Klein, Alyson. (2015). Education week: The nation's main K–12 law at 50. *Education Week.* Retrieved from http://www.edweek.org/ew/section/multimedia/the-nations-main-k-12-law-a-timeline.html

Latunde, Yvette, & Clark-Louque, Angela R. (2016). Untapped resources: Black parent engagement that contributes to learning. *The Journal of Negro Education, 85*(1), 72–81.

Lau v. Nichols, 483 F.2d 791 (9th Cir. 1973); 414 U.S. 563 (1974).

Lawlor, K. Blaine, & Hornyak, Martin. (2012). SMART Goals: How the application of SMART goals can contribute to the achievement of student learning outcomes. *Developments in Business Simulation and Experiential Learning Journal, 39*, 259–267.

Leadership Conference Education Fund. (2017, May). *The 2nd annual new education majority poll: Black and Latino parents and families on education and their children's future.* www.leadershipconferenceedfund.org

Lee, Valerie, & Smith, Julia B. (1996). Collective responsibility for learning and its effects on gains in achievement for early secondary school students. *American Journal of Education, 104*(2), 103–147.

Lezotte, Lawrence. (1997). *Learning for all.* Okemos, MI: Effective Schools Product.

Lindsey, Delores B., Terrell, Raymond D., Nuri, Kikanza J., & Lindsey, Randall B. (2010). Focus on assets, overcome barriers. *Leadership, 39*(5), 12–15.

Lindsey, Delores B., Thousand, Jacqueline S., Jew, Cynthia L., & Piowlski, Lori R. (2018). *Culturally proficient inclusive schools: All means all!* Thousand Oaks, CA: Corwin.

Lindsey, Randall B., Nuri-Robins, Kikanza, Terrell, Raymond D., & Lindsey, Delores B. (2018). *Cultural proficiency: A manual for school leaders* (4th ed.). Thousand Oaks, CA: Corwin.

Louis, Karen S., Murphy, Joseph, & Smylie, Mark. (2016). Caring leadership in schools: Findings from exploratory analyses. *Educational Administration Quarterly, 52*(2), 310–334.

Louque, Angela, & Latunde, Yvette. (2014). Cultural capital in the village: The role Black families play in the education of children. *Journal of Multicultural Education, 21*(3/4), 5–10.

Mapp, Karen. (2003). Having their say: Parents describe how and why they are engaged in their children's learning. *School Community Journal, 13*(1), 35–64.

Mapp, Karen. (2018). *Family engagement in education: Creating effective home and school partnerships for student success.* https://www.gse.harvard.edu/ppe/program/family-engagement-education-creating-effective-home-and-school-partnerships-student

Mapp, Karen, & Kuttner, Paul. (2013). *Partners in Education: A Dual-Capacity Building Framework for Family, School Partnerships.* SEDL and the US Department of Education. https://www2.ed.gov/documents/family-community/partners-education.pdf

Mazzone, Nora M., & Miglionico, Barbara J. (2014). *Stress-busting strategies for teachers: How do I manage the pressures of teaching?* Alexandria, VA: Association of Supervision and Curriculum Development.

Mendez v. Westminster School District of Orange County. (1947). 161 F.2d 774 (9th Cir. 1947).

Moore, Edward, Bagin, Don, & Gallegher, Don. (2012). *The school and community relations.* London: Pearson.

Morrison, Mike. (2010). History of SMART objectives. *Rapid Business Improvement.* Retrieved from http://rapidbi.com/management/history-of-smart-objectives/

National Association for Family, School, and Community Engagement (NAFSCE). (2009). https://nafsce.org

National Board for Professional Teaching Standards. (2016). *What teachers should know and be able to do.* http://accomplishedteacher.org/wp-content/uploads/2016/12/NBPTS-What-Teachers-Should-Know-and-Be-Able-to-Do-.pdf

National Center for Education Statistics. (2014). *The condition of education 2014.* US Department of Education. https://nces.ed.gov/pubs2014/2014083.pdf

National Commission on Excellence in Education. (1983). *A nation at risk: The imperative for educational reform, a report to the nation and the secretary of education, US Department of Education.* The Commission.

National Family, School, and Community Engagement Working Group. (2009). Retrieved from http://hfrp.org/family-involvement/projects/national/family-school

National Policy Board for Educational Administration. (2015). *Professional standards for educational leaders 2015.* Reston, VA: Author.

New York State Education Department. (2011). New York State Teaching Standards. https://www.engageny.org/resource/new-york-state-teaching-standards

Nieto, Sonia, & Bode, Patty. (2012). *Affirming diversity: The sociopolitical context of multicultural education* (6th ed.). Boston, MA: Pearson Education.

No Child Left Behind Act of 2001, P.L. 107-110, 20 U. S. C. § 6319 (2002).

Noddings, Nel. (1992). *The challenge to care in schools: An alternative approach to education.* New York, NY: Teachers College Press.

Noddings, Nel. (2005). 'Caring in education,' the encyclopedia of informal information. www.infed.org/biblio/noddings_caring_in_education.htm

O'Brien, Anne. (2017). *What do parents want from schools? Key takeaways from four recent polls that asked parents and guardians for their thoughts on education.* https://www.edutopia.org/article/what-do-parents-want-schools

Olender, Rosemary, Elias, Jacquelyn, & Mastroleo, Rosemary. (2010). *School-home connections: Forging positive relationships with parents.* Thousand Oaks, CA: Corwin.

Orfield, Gary, & Frankenberg, Elizabeth. (2007). *Lessons in integration: Realizing the promise of racial diversity in America's public schools.* Charlottesville: University of Virginia Press.

Paredes, Maria. (2011). Parent involvement as an instructional strategy: Academic Parent-Teacher Teams. Unpublished dissertation. Arizona State University. https://repository.asu.edu/attachments/56346/content/Paredes_asu_0010E_10305.pdf

Paredes, Maria. (2015). APTT: Intentional and strategic family engagement. A project of WestEd. Webinar, p. 6. http://iel.org/sites/default/files/APTT%20Chicago%20June%20 2015.pdf

Patient Protection and Affordable Care Act. (2010). *Maternal, Infant, and Early Childhood Visiting (MIECHV) Program.* Pub. L. No. 111-148.

Pub. L. No. 94-142. (1975).

Pushor, Debbie [@DrDebbiePushor]. (2018, November 27) #parentengagement [Tweet]. Retrieved from https://twitter.com/drdebbiepushor?lang=en

Quezada, Reyes L. (2014). Family-school, & community engagement and partnerships: Working with culturally diverse families. *Multicultural Education, 21*(3/4), 2.

Quezada, Reyes L., Alexandrowicz, Viviana, & Molina, Sarina. (Eds.). (2015). *Family, school community engagement and partnerships: An imperative for K–12, and colleges of education in the development of 21st century educators.* UK: Routledge.

Reform Support Network. (2014, March). Strategies for community engagement in school turnaround. US Department of Education. https://www2.ed.gov/about/inits/ed/implementation-support-unit/tech-assist/strategies-for-community-engagement-in-school-turnaround.pdf

Riehl, Carolyn J. (2000). The principal's role in creating inclusive schools for diverse students: A review of normative, empirical, and critical literature on the practice of educational administration. *Review of Educational Research, 70*(1), 55–81.

Senge, Peter M., Cambron-McCabe, Nelda H., Lucas, Timothy, Kleiner, Art, Dutton, Janis, & Smith, Bryan. (2000). *Schools that learn: A fifth discipline fieldbook for educators, parents, and everyone who cares about education.* New York, NY: Doubleday.

Serrano v. Priest, 5 Cal. 3d 584, 487 P.2d 1241, 96 Cal. Rptr 601 (1971).

Shapiro, Joan Poliner, & Stefkovich, Jacqueline A. (2016). *Ethical leadership and decision making in education.* New York: Routledge. https//doi.org/10.4324/9781315773339

Sotomayer, Sonia. (2013). *My beloved world.* New York, NY: Random House, Inc.

Southern Education Foundation. (2017). *A new majority: Low-income students in the south & nation.* https://www.southerneducation.org/what-we-do/research/pre-k-12-education/

Strarrat, Robert J. (1994). *Building an ethical school: A practical response to the moral crisis in schools.* London: Routledge.

Tennessee Professional Teaching Standards. (n.d.). http://ww2.nscc.edu/depart/docs/educ/pdf/TN-Professional-Teaching-Standards.pdf

Terrell, Raymond, & Lindsey, Randall. (2009). *Culturally proficient leadership: The personal journey begins within.* Thousand Oaks, CA: Corwin.

Thompson, Gail. (2002). *African American teens discuss their schooling experiences.* Westport, CT: Greenwood Publishing.

Thompson, Gail. (2003). *What African American parents want educators to know*. Westport, CT: Greenwood Publishing.

Ujifusa, Andrew. (2016). Funding flexibility enhanced under new K–12 law. *Education Week*. Retrieved from http://www.edweek.org/ew/articles/2016/01/06/funding-flexibility-enhanced-under-new-k-12-law.html

Ulmer, Kenneth C. (2018). *Passing the generation blessing: Speak life, shape destinies*. Franklin, TN: Worthy Publishing.

US Department of Education. (2016). Toolkit of resources for engaging families and the community as partners in education: Part I. Building an understanding of family and community engagement.

US Department of State. (2019). Chapter 5: Collaboration. https://www.state.gov/m/a/os/43980.htm

Vanzant, Iyanla. (2001). *Faith in the valley: Lessons for women on the journey to peace*. New York, NY: Simon & Schuster.

Villa, Richard, & Thousand, Jacqueline. (2017). *Leading an inclusive school: Access and success for ALL students*. Alexandria, VA: ASCD.

Villa, Richard, Thousand, Jacqueline, & Nevin, Ann I. (2013). *A guide to co-teaching: New lessons and strategies to facilitate student learning* (3rd ed.). Thousand Oaks, CA: Corwin.

Villani, Christine J. (1999). Community culture and school climate. *The School Community Journal, 9*(1), 103–105.

Warren, Mark R., Hong, Soo, Rubin, Carolyn Leung, & Uy, Phitsamay Sychitkokhong. (2009). Beyond the bake sale: A community-based relational approach to parent engagement in schools. *Teachers College Record, 111*(9), 2209–2254.

Weaver, S. (2017). *Most families say ongoing communication supports student learning*. http://flamboyanfoundation.org/2017/07/06/most-families-say-ongoing-communication-supports-student-learning/

Weiss, Heather B., Bouffard, Suzanne M., Bridglall, Beatrice L., and Gordon, Edmund W. (2009). *Reframing family involvement in education: Supporting families to support educational equity*. Teachers College, Columbia University.

Weiss, Heather, Lopez, M. Elena, & Rosenberg, Heidi. (2010). *Beyond random acts: Family, school, and community engagement as an integral part of education reform*. Harvard Family Research Project.

Weller, David L., & Weller, Sylvia J. (2002). *Assistant principal: Essentials for effective school leadership*. Thousand Oaks, CA: Corwin.

Weyer, Matt. (2015). Engaging families in education. National Conference of State Legislatures. http://www.ncsl.org/Portals/1/Documents/educ/Engaging_Families_Education.pdf

Whalan, Frances. (2012) *Collective responsibility: Redefining what falls between the cracks for school reform*. Boston, MA: Sense Publishers.

Wiggington, Eliot. (1972). *Sometimes a shining moment: The foxfire experience. Twenty years teaching in a high school classroom*. New York, NY: Anchor Books, Random House.

Winfrey, Oprah. (2011, June). One incredible journey. *O, the Oprah Magazine, 12*, 6.

Yousafzai, Malala. (2016). *I am Malala: The girl who stood up for education and was shot by the Taliban*. Martin's Lane, London: Orion Publishing Group Ltd.

Zarate, Maria. (2007). *Understanding Latino parental involvement in education: Perceptions, expectations, and recommendation*. Tomas Rivera Policy Institute, University of Southern California.

Index

CORWIN

A SAGE Publishing Company

Helping educators make the greatest impact

CORWIN HAS ONE MISSION: to enhance education through intentional professional learning.

We build long-term relationships with our authors, educators, clients, and associations who partner with us to develop and continuously improve the best evidence-based practices that establish and support lifelong learning.

Solutions YOU WANT | Experts YOU TRUST | Results YOU NEED

EVENTS >>> **INSTITUTES**

Corwin Institutes provide large regional events where educators collaborate with peers and learn from industry experts. Prepare to be recharged and motivated!

corwin.com/institutes

ON-SITE PD >>> **ON-SITE PROFESSIONAL LEARNING**

Corwin on-site PD is delivered through high-energy keynotes, practical workshops, and custom coaching services designed to support knowledge development and implementation.

corwin.com/pd

>>> **PROFESSIONAL DEVELOPMENT RESOURCE CENTER**

The PD Resource Center provides school and district PD facilitators with the tools and resources needed to deliver effective PD.

corwin.com/pdrc

ONLINE >>> **ADVANCE**

Designed for K–12 teachers, Advance offers a range of online learning options that can qualify for graduate-level credit and apply toward license renewal.

corwin.com/advance

Contact a PD Advisor at (800) 831-6640 or visit www.corwin.com for more information